Revised

Exploring English 6

Dr K. Padmini Shankar

The publishers would like to thank the following for their suggestions and inputs:

English Department
Nowgong Mission High School
Nagaon, Assam

Sister (Dr) Molly Kaniampadickal
St Mary's Higher Secondary School
Guwahati, Assam

English Department
Little Flower Higher Secondary School
Dibrugarh, Assam

English Department
St Joseph's Convent Higher Secondary School
Tezpur, Assam

Balwinder Deol
Head of the Department, English
Mount St Mary's School, New Delhi

Portia Benazir
Head of the Department, English
Howard Public School, Hyderabad

Collins

Revised

Exploring English 6

K. Padmini Shankar

Published by Collins India
A division of HarperCollins*Publishers* India Private Limited
HarperCollins *Publishers*
A-75, Sector 57, Noida, Uttar Pradesh 201301, India
1 London Bridge Street, London, SE1 9GF, United Kingdom
2 Bloor Street East, Toronto, Ontario M4W 1A8, Canada
Lvl 13, 201 Elizabeth Street (PO Box A565, NSW, 1235),
Sydney NSW 2000, Australia
195 Broadway, New York, NY 10007, USA

Browse the complete Collins catalogue at
www.collins.in

First edition 2015
Latest revised edition 2018

Reprint: 10 9

ISBN: 978-93-5277-139-4

Typesetting and page layout by Q2A Media Services Private Limited, Recto Graphics

Cover layout by Rahul Dhiman

Printed and bound in India by Thomson Press India Ltd

ACKNOWLEDGEMENTS

The publishers wish to thank and acknowledge the following for granting us permission to use copyright material:

Valerie Allen for *Baby's Ears* from *Chicken Soup for the Kid's Soul* by Jack Canfield, Mark Victor Hansen, Patty Hansen, and Irene Dunlap. Copyright 2012 by Chicken Soup for the Soul Publishing, LLC. Published by Backlist, LLC, a unit of Chicken Soup for the Soul Publishing, LLC. Chicken Soup for the Soul is a registered trademark of Chicken Soup for the Soul Publishing, LLC. Reprinted by permission. All rights reserved. Anthony Matthews for *Feline Eating Disorders* from www.dearcustomerrelations.com; Gareth Owen for *Dear Mr Examiner*, printed with permission of Rogers. Coleridge & White Literary Agency; Michael Morpurgo for *The Butterfly Lion* (HarperCollins Publishers); *Seventeen Oranges* from *Goalkeeper's Revenge* by Bill Naughton, reprinted by permission of Peters Fraser & Dunlop (www.petersfraserdunlop.com) on behalf of the Estate of Bill Naughton; Matthew Sweeney for *Fishbones Dreaming* from *Up on the Roof: New and Selected Poems* copyright © Matthew Sweeney and reprinted by permission of Faber and Faber Ltd; Milkha Singh and Sonia Sanwalka for *The Flying Sikh* from *The Race of My Life*, reproduced by permission of Rupa Publications India; Sigrun Srivastav for *The Take-Off Board* from *Heroes Never Die and Other Stories*, published by Puffin Books, Penguin Books, India; Terry Bisson for *They're Made Out Of Meat*. Copyright © 1990 by Terry Bisson, Reprinted by permission of Terry Bisson; Loreen Leedy for *The Bad Old Days* from *My Teacher Is a Dinosaur: And Other Prehistoric Poems, Jokes, Riddles & Amazing Facts* copyright © Loreen Leedy 2010 by permission of Amazon Publishing.

The publishers have applied for permission for *The Future* from the *Pachamama*. Acknowledgments for the passage will be made in the future editions of the book.

Every effort has been made to trace copyright holders and to obtain their permission for the use of copyright material. However, in some instances, we have been unable to trace the owners of the copyright pieces published here. The authors and publishers will gladly receive any information enabling them to rectify any error or omission in subsequent editions.

Illustrations

Unit 1: *Rescue Poem*, Amit John; Unit 2: *My Failed Omelettes and Other Disasters* and *The Lumberjack and the Tree*, Sayantan Halder; Unit 3: *The Butterfly Lion*, Amit John; *The Future*, Sayantan Halder; Unit 4: *Fishbones Dreaming*, Amit John; p97: Richa Kinra; Unit 5: *The Take-off Board*, Amit John; *One Look*, Sebin Simon; Unit 6: *Science Fiction or Science Facts?*, Sebin Simon; *The Time Machine*, Amit John. All other illustrations Q2A Media Services Private Limited, Danish Zaidi.

Photographs

p12: Per-Anders Pettersson/Corbis; p13: Neftali; p14: Louise Gubb/CORBIS SABA; p24: Milorad Zaric; p29: cirodelia; p30: Askold Romanov; p31: Andrew_Howe, shibanuk, danilo sanino; p37: filo; p46: RussellCreative, TheaVector; p48: Leonhartrizal; p51: CandO_Designs; p64: MR1805 p71: strelss; p72: &#169 Claudelle Girard, ilbusca, &#169 jamesbenet, CSA-Images, Multipedia, ddraw; p73: John1179; p76: rod2334; p91: DeShoff, Darumo; p102: The LIFE Picture Collection; p103: ©ZUMA Press, Inc./Alamy; p106: cako74; p115: mitza; p116: kbeis; p117: duescreatius1; p127: Valeriy Kachaev; p128: ilyast; p137: CSA-Printstock; p139: tharrison.

KEY TO ICONS

The **book** icon indicates the beginning of each reading passage.

The **audio** icon indicates a listening activity.

VBQ The **VBQ** tab indicates value-based questions.

PREFACE

Revised Exploring English is a multi-skill course in English, designed for children and young people growing up in a world of global communications. It aims to develop their cognitive abilities, train them to think critically and communicate effectively in a wide variety of contexts. It adheres to the latest National Curriculum Framework. The series has been revised and updated based on detailed user feedback.

Built around salient themes, the units in the book comprise carefully selected reading texts authored by Indian and global writers. They cater to a variety of student interests and needs, motivate engagement and promote critical thinking. Through the reading of the texts, learners are expected to develop as thinking individuals who are keenly aware of the world around them – linguistically competent, cognitively able, and morally responsible.

The eight-level series includes coursebooks, workbooks and literature readers for levels 3 to 8. Each level is also accompanied by a comprehensive Teacher's Resource Book and digital resources for the teacher in the form of an interactive DVD.

Coursebooks 6–8

Each unit in Books 6–8 includes a non-fiction prose passage, a fictional text and a poem. A unit comprises the following components:

- Warm-up: includes tasks which stimulate the learner's interest in the theme of the unit.
- Reading 1: a factual piece that introduces the topic and motivates students to explore further. The information-rich texts cover a variety of contemporary writing genres, including reviews, authentic reports, journalistic articles, autobiographical pieces and travelogues. The contextual glossary helps learners with difficult or literary words.
- Comprehension 1: comprises factual questions that encourage close reading as well as scanning for specific details, and ensure a thorough understanding of the information in the text.
- Comprehension 2: comprises inferential, evaluative and value-based questions that develop higher order thinking skills by encouraging learners to analyse the facts of the story and to draw parallels between events in the text and their own experiences.
- Vocabulary check: includes activities which ensure that learners understand key words in the text.
- Language skills: covers areas such as pronunciation, spelling and punctuation that give learners the edge in making their speech more fluent and their writing more accurate. Components such as dictionary work also encourage learner autonomy.
- Reading 2: a fictional piece, such as a short story or an extract from a novel. These include both classic and contemporary texts. It is also followed by Comprehension 1 and Comprehension 2.
- Vocabulary: the tasks here check the learner's understanding of useful vocabulary in the story, and provide extension exercises based on the theme of the unit.
- Grammar: includes a short application-based explanation of concepts, illustrated through contextual examples, and followed by tasks which provide extensive practice. The exercises are graded, ensuring that the learner moves from simpler tasks to more practical applications.
- Listening: related to the theme of the unit and presented in authentic contexts, it includes activities which provide practice in listening for both specific and general meaning, as well as in identifying vocabulary and grammar topics already taught in the unit.
- Speaking: includes individual, pair and group work for practising spoken English related to the theme of the unit. Prompts and useful phrases give learners a springboard for the tasks, providing practice in English that they will be able to use in real-life situations.

- Writing: includes guided and free writing tasks derived from the reading text, which encourage creativity while enabling learners to create a meaningful and fluent piece of text.
- Poems: these have been carefully chosen to appeal to learners, with questions that range from the factual to the interpretative. It is followed by an activity loosely related to the theme of the poem.

Projects: include creative and research-based activities which encourage teamwork.

Life skills: built around values and skills, it consists of tasks that equip learners to deal with real-life situations as balanced individuals.

Workbooks

The Workbooks are designed to complement the Coursebooks through the careful mapping of grammar and vocabulary, with additional practice to review and reinforce concepts. The grammar sections include a short reminder of the grammar point covered in the Coursebook. Further practice in comprehension, vocabulary, language skills and writing is also provided.

Literature Readers

The Literature Readers teach critical appreciation of literature through short stories, folktales and fairytales, extracts from quality literature and classic novels, and poems from various eras and regions. A range of text-types is covered, with learners' attention being drawn to the genre of each piece. Literary devices are also highlighted, with a glossary of literary terms at the end of each book.

Teacher's Resource Books

The Teacher's Resource Books contain model lesson plans, photocopiable worksheets covering all the pedagogical aspects included in the Coursebooks, answer keys to all exercises, along with extra analytical activity sheets.

Digital resources

The Collins DigiSuite DVD comprises:

1. **Enhanced e-book:** includes the coursebook in digital format with additional features like audio, animated poems, pronunciation help and interactive exercises.
2. **Test generator:** an easy-to-use tool to help teachers create tests with a few clicks.
3. **Teacher resources:** includes lesson plans, answer keys, listening texts, additional worksheets, further project ideas, and extra support with assessment.

We hope that the course will foster a love for reading in young learners and provide teachers with language acquisition tools that can be used to effectively impart communication skills and equip young minds with an awareness about the world.

Dr K. Padmini Shankar, Series Editor

KEY FEATURES

In this unit, I will ... lists the learning objectives for the unit.

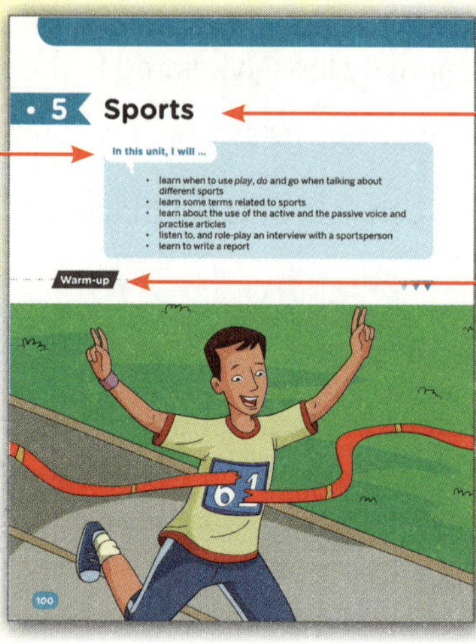

Each unit is built around a **theme**.

Warm-up has activities related to the theme of the unit.

Each unit covers texts belonging to a rich variety of genres, by Indian and international authors. **Reading 1** includes a non-fiction prose text. **Reading 2** includes a fictional prose text.

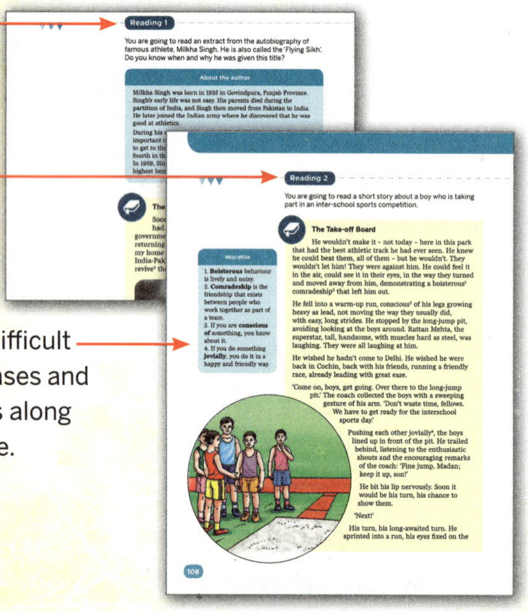

Wordfile lists difficult words and phrases and gives meanings along with their usage.

Both Reading sections are followed by exercises. **Comprehension 1** checks factual understanding through gap-filling, multiple choice, reference to context as well as 'wh-' questions.

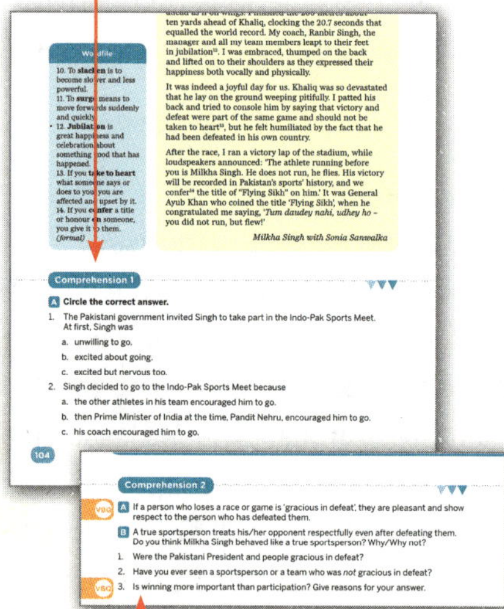

Comprehension 2 checks analytical, evaluative, inferential and interpretative skills. It also includes value-based questions, indicated by an icon.

Each unit also includes a **Poem** followed by **Poetry appreciation** and an **Activity** related to the poem.

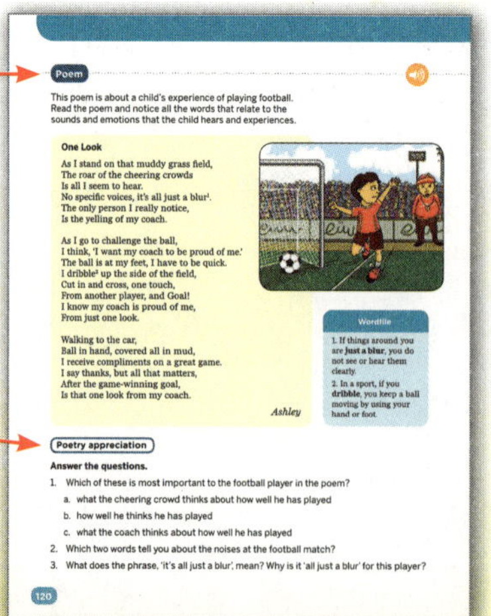

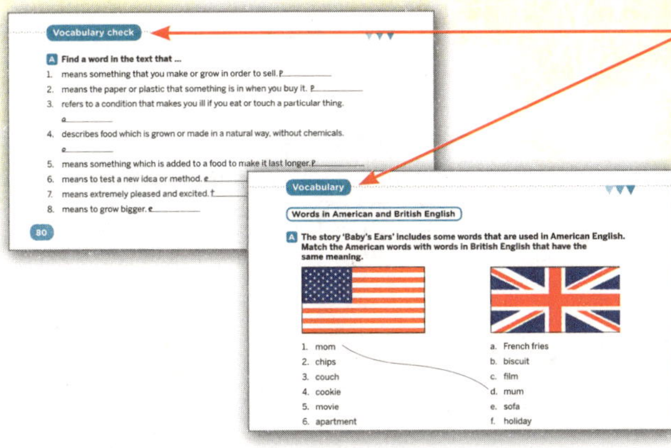

Vocabulary check

A Find a word in the text that ...

1. means something that you make or grow in order to sell. f
2. means the paper or plastic that something is in when you buy it. p
3. refers to a condition that makes you ill if you eat or touch a particular thing. a
4. describes food which is grown or made in a natural way, without chemicals. o
5. means something which is added to a food to make it last longer. p
6. means to test a new idea or method. e
7. means extremely pleased and excited. t
8. means to grow bigger. e

80

Vocabulary

Words in American and British English

A The story 'Baby's Ears' includes some words that are used in American English. Match the American words with words in British English that have the same meaning.

1. mom	a. French fries
2. chips	b. biscuit
3. couch	c. film
4. cookie	d. mum
5. movie	e. sofa
6. apartment	f. holiday

Vocabulary check and **Vocabulary** enrich the learner's language.

Language skills encourages the use of dictionaries and focuses on phonics and spelling.

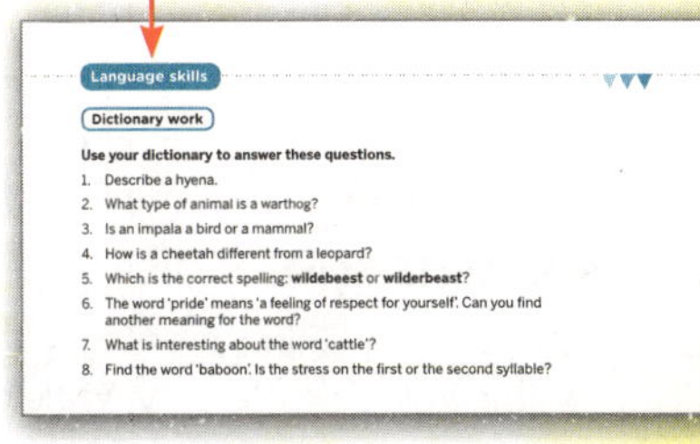

Language skills

Dictionary work

Use your dictionary to answer these questions.

1. Describe a hyena.
2. What type of animal is a warthog?
3. Is an impala a bird or a mammal?
4. How is a cheetah different from a leopard?
5. Which is the correct spelling: **wildebeest** or **wilderbeast**?
6. The word 'pride' means 'a feeling of respect for yourself'. Can you find another meaning for the word?
7. What is interesting about the word 'cattle'?
8. Find the word 'baboon'. Is the stress on the first or the second syllable?

Grammar builds language proficiency through communicative and usage-based tasks.

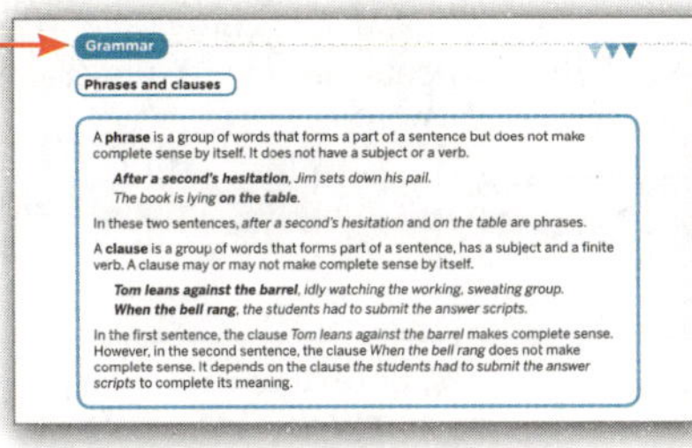

Grammar

Phrases and clauses

A **phrase** is a group of words that forms a part of a sentence but does not make complete sense by itself. It does not have a subject or a verb.

After a second's hesitation, Jim sets down his pail.
The book is lying on the table.

In these two sentences, *after a second's hesitation* and *on the table* are phrases.

A **clause** is a group of words that forms part of a sentence, has a subject and a finite verb. A clause may or may not make complete sense by itself.

Tom leans against the barrel, idly watching the working, sweating group.
When the bell rang, the students had to submit the answer scripts.

In the first sentence, the clause *Tom leans against the barrel* makes complete sense. However, in the second sentence, the clause *When the bell rang* does not make complete sense. It depends on the clause *the students had to submit the answer scripts* to complete its meaning.

Writing tasks help the students develop their imaginative and critical thinking abilities, and challenge them to explore new ways of expressing themselves effectively and creatively.

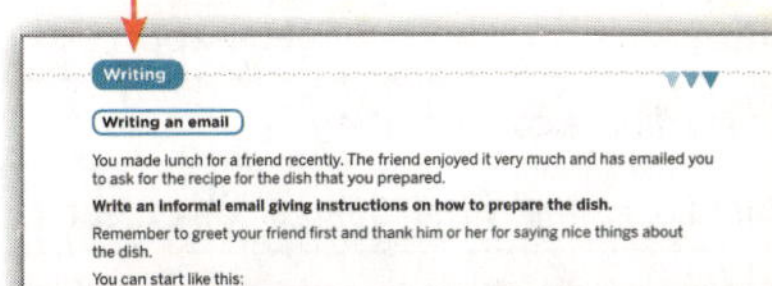

Writing

Writing an email

You made lunch for a friend recently. The friend enjoyed it very much and has emailed you to ask for the recipe for the dish that you prepared.

Write an informal email giving instructions on how to prepare the dish.

Remember to greet your friend first and thank him or her for saying nice things about the dish.

You can start like this:

Listening and **Speaking** exercises focus on honing oral and aural skills through listening comprehension, group discussions and role plays.

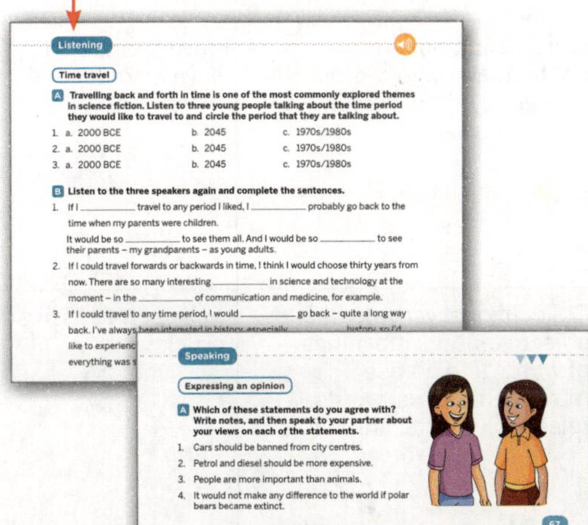

Listening

Time travel

A Travelling back and forth in time is one of the most commonly explored themes in science fiction. Listen to three young people talking about the time period they would like to travel to and circle the period that they are talking about.

1. a. 2000 BCE b. 2045 c. 1970s/1980s
2. a. 2000 BCE b. 2045 c. 1970s/1980s
3. a. 2000 BCE b. 2045 c. 1970s/1980s

B Listen to the three speakers again and complete the sentences.

1. If I ______ travel to any period I liked, I ______ probably go back to the time when my parents were children. It would be so ______ to see them all. And I would be so ______ to see their parents – my grandparents – as young adults.
2. If I could travel forwards or backwards in time, I think I would choose thirty years from now. There are so many interesting ______ in science and technology at the moment – in the ______ of communication and medicine, for example.
3. If I could travel to any time period, I would ______ go back – quite a long way back. I've always ...

Speaking

Expressing an opinion

A Which of these statements do you agree with? Write notes, and then speak to your partner about your views on each of the statements.

1. Cars should be banned from city centres.
2. Petrol and diesel should be more expensive.
3. People are more important than animals.
4. It would not make any difference to the world if polar bears became extinct.

67

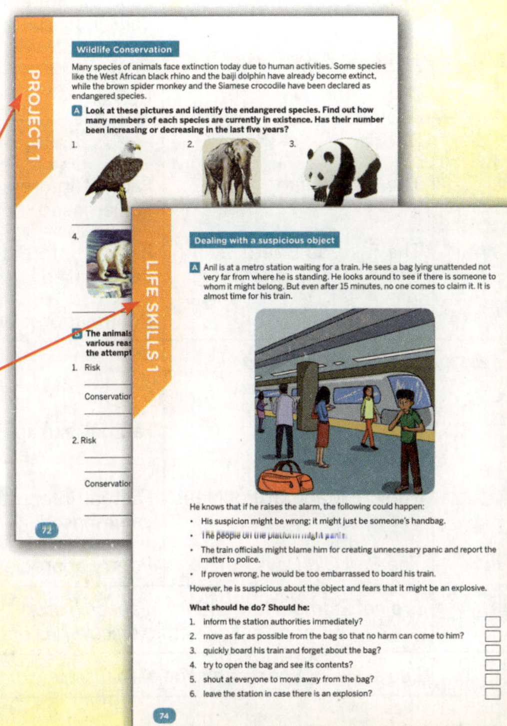

PROJECT 1

Wildlife Conservation

Many species of animals face extinction today due to human activities. Some species like the West African black rhino and the baiji dolphin have already become extinct, while the brown spider monkey and the Siamese crocodile have been declared as endangered species.

A Look at these pictures and identify the endangered species. Find out how many members of each species are currently in existence. Has their number been increasing or decreasing in the last five years?

72

LIFE SKILLS 1

Dealing with a suspicious object

A Anil is at a metro station waiting for a train. He sees a bag lying unattended not very far from where he is standing. He looks around to see if there is someone to whom it might belong. But even after 15 minutes, no one comes to claim it. It is almost time for his train.

He knows that if he raises the alarm, the following could happen:

- His suspicion might be wrong; it might just be someone's handbag.
- The people on the platform might panic.
- The train officials might blame him for creating unnecessary panic and report the matter to police.
- If proven wrong, he would be too embarrassed to board his train.

However, he is suspicious about the object and fears that it might be an explosive.

What should he do? Should he:

1. inform the station authorities immediately?
2. move as far as possible from the bag so that no harm can come to him?
3. quickly board his train and forget about the bag?
4. try to open the bag and see its contents?
5. shout at everyone to move away from the bag?
6. leave the station in case there is an explosion?

74

Project and **Life skills** pages encourage group work. They help students imbibe values and attitudes required to overcome challenges in real life.

CONTENTS MAP

Unit	Title	Reading Comprehension	Vocabulary	Grammar
1	**People Who Do Good for Others**		Idiomatic phrases; American English and British English	Simple past and past continuous tense; subject and predicate
	Hero: Nelson Mandela, an End to Injustice?	Factual, inferential, extrapolative, value-based		
	Baby's Ears	Factual, inferential, extrapolative, value based		
	Rescue Poem	Poetry appreciation		
2	**Amusing Incidents**		Fill in the blanks: contextual usage; proverbs related to cats; antonyms; unscrambling words	Phrases and clauses
	Feline Eating Disorders	Factual, inferential, extrapolative, value based		
	Tom Paints the Fence	Factual, inferential, extrapolative, value based		
	Dear Mr Examiner	Poetry appreciation		
3	**The Environment**		Contextual vocabulary; compound words; verbs related to animal movements	Phrasal verbs with and without an object
	Save Our World	Factual, extrapolative, value-based		
	The Butterfly Lion	Factual, inferential, extrapolative, value based		
	The Future	Poetry appreciation		
	Project 1: Wildlife conservation			
	Life skills 1: Dealing with a suspicious object			
4	**Food**		Word definitions; verbs: contextual usage; words related to crime; crossword	*Have to* and *don't have to*; *must* and *mustn't*
	Zach's Story	Factual, extrapolative, value-based		
	Seventeen Oranges	Factual, inferential, extrapolative, value based		
	Fishbones Dreaming	Poetry appreciation Refrain		
5	**Sports**		Collocations: verb-noun and adjective-noun; meanings of words and phrases; movement words; words related to sports; antonyms	Active and passive voice; articles
	The Flying Sikh	Factual, inferential, extrapolative, value-based		
	The Take-off Board	Factual, inferential, extrapolative, value based		
	One Look	Poetry appreciation		
6	**Looking Back and Looking Forwards**		Contextual vocabulary; homonyms; parts of speech	The second conditional: prepositions
	Science Fiction or Science Facts?	Factual, extrapolative, value-based		
	They're Made Out of Meat	Factual, inferential, extrapolative, value-based		
	The Bad Old Days	Poetry appreciation		
	Project 2: Important events in space history *Important scientific discoveries of the twentieth century*			
	Life skills 2 : Sports and sportsmanship			

Language skills	Listening	Speaking	Writing	Activity
Pronunciation: syllables and word stress	Listening to a conversation on making requests and choosing the correct answer, and gap filling	Role play: asking people politely to do something; practising agreeing and refusing	Descriptive writing: creating an atmosphere in the opening paragraphs of a story	Gathering information about animal welfare organizations and completing a table; making a poster
Punctuation: hyphens and dashes	Listening to a passage and answering questions; listening to a passage and gap filling	Pair work: enacting given situations Conducting a group discussion on a topic followed by a presentation	Writing about an embarrassing incident	Writing an acrostic poem
Dictionary work: words related to animals	Listening to a passage and marking true or false and completing sentences	Role play: expressing an opinion Pair work: preparing and giving a speech on a given topic	Writing a letter describing a holiday	Making a presentation on the problem of air pollution in your city
Idioms with *word*; pronunciation: *have to* and *has to*	Listening to a passage and choosing the correct answer, and gap filling	Pair work: preparing a short speech on a given topic	Writing an email and sharing a recipe	Categorizing food items Preparing a calorie chart
Dictionary work: using *play*, *do*, *go* in sports and leisure activities	Listening to an interview and answering questions, and gap filling	Pair work: interviewing someone using the phrases given	Writing a report of a sporting event for the school magazine	Gathering information about the 2016 Olympic Games
Prefixes and suffixes	Listening to a passage and choosing the correct answer and gap filling	Speaking on a given topic using the phrases given	Writing a diary entry after travelling to another planet	Writing a paragraph on a scientific invention

CONTENTS

1 People Who Do Good for Others

In this unit, I will ...

- learn about syllables and word stress
- learn about differences between American and British English
- learn about uses of the simple past and the past continuous and practise subject and predicate
- practise making polite requests
- write the opening section of a story

Warm-up

A **What are these people doing? Look at these six pictures and discuss with your partner how one person is helping another.**

1. 

2. 

3. 

4. 

5. 

6. 

B **What are some other situations in which people might need help? How can we help them?**

Reading 1

Nelson Mandela was the first black President of South Africa. He is remembered today for his long struggle to bring justice to black South Africans, who faced cruelty and discrimination at the hands of the whites. Read on to find out more about him.

Hero: Nelson Mandela, an End to Injustice?

'Friends, comrades[1] and fellow South Africans!

I greet you all in the name of peace, democracy[2] and freedom for all. Your tireless and heroic sacrifices[3] have made it possible for me to be here today. I therefore place the remaining years of my life in your hands.'

These words welcomed hundreds of thousands of cheering black South Africans who gathered in the streets of Cape Town on 11 February 1990. They were there to salute their hero, Madiba, as they lovingly called him, after his release from prison, where he had spent 27 years of his life. His real name was Nelson Rolihlahla Mandela, and his freedom marked one of the most important events in the history of South Africa – the beginning of the end of injustice, inequality and discrimination.

Nelson Mandela was born on 18 July 1918 in Umtau in South Africa. Neither of his parents ever went to school, but they ensured that Mandela did. He, like his father, had a deep sense of justice, and this quality played a key role in his later career as a political revolutionary[4]. He was only nine when his father died. From then onwards,

Wordfile

1. A person's **comrades** are friends that they have fought together with.
2. **Democracy** is a system of government in which people choose their leaders by voting for them in elections.
3. A **sacrifice** is something important that you stop having or doing in order to get something else for yourself or for another person.
4. A **revolutionary** is someone who tries to change their country's government by using force.

it was his mother who was responsible for the wellbeing and education of the children. At school, his teacher, Miss Mdingane (pronounced 'Mmm-ding-ga-nay'), gave him the English name 'Nelson'. He took a lot of interest in studies but was equally active in sports, his favourites being boxing and athletics.

When Mandela went to university, he was the only local African student there, and he faced a lot of discrimination[5] because of his skin colour. The black South Africans, though greater in number, had almost no rights in the country. They were oppressed[6], insulted and often treated inhumanely[7] by white people[8]. The National Party came into power in 1948, and the situation became much worse. The party supported the separation of black and white South Africans. The saddest thing was that those black people who already had a powerful position in society took the side of the whites, and they spoke in favour of the separation of the common black people. This was the birth of 'apartheid'[9], a word that comes from the Afrikaans[10] language, and means 'being separate or apart'. For thousands of black South Africans, their own motherland became a living hell.

Mandela's deep sense of justice and his belief in the rights of the common people made him actively participate in political protests against apartheid. He was unable to finish his studies at the university because he was against many of the university's policies. He was asked to leave. From as early as 1952, he was an important member of the African National Congress, a party that fought for the rights of the common people. He devoted himself to political campaigns and rallies, and made speeches against the injustice and discrimination faced by his people. He had taken upon himself a very difficult and dangerous responsibility, but he remained fearless and devoted to his cause till the very end.

After being forced to give up his degree, Mandela moved to Johannesburg. In order to support himself, he started working as a security guard at a mine. Soon, one of his more successful friends helped Mandela get a job at a law firm, as an accountant. Mandela had always understood the importance of education in life and so, while working at the law firm, he once again enrolled[11] for a Bachelor's degree, and this time successfully completed it. It was

Wordfile

5. **Discrimination** is the practice of treating one person or group in a way that is not fair.
6. To **oppress** people means to treat them cruelly or to stop them from having the same freedom as other people.
7. If you treat someone **inhumanely**, you treat that person in a very cruel way.
8. **White people** belong to a race of people with a pale skin.
9. In the past, **apartheid** was a political system in South Africa, in which people of different races were kept separate by law. It is pronounced 'apartite'.
10. **Afrikaans** is a language that is spoken in South Africa.
11. If you **enrol**, you officially join a class.

during these years in Johannesburg that Mandela became more deeply involved in politics and joined revolutionary groups that were fighting for the rights of the common black people. In the beginning, Mandela and those with him followed in Gandhi's footsteps, believing in the power of non-violence. However, as the years went by, it became clear to them that they would not be able to win without armed struggle[12]. Much later, Mandela said that taking up arms was the last option, and they were forced to adopt violent ways of protesting against apartheid because of the violence they themselves faced every day.

From 1960, the protests became increasingly violent with bomb explosions, strikes and clashes between the police and the protesters. Finally, in 1962, Nelson Mandela was arrested and charged for being a part of the protests against the ruling government. He was sent to prison and remained there for twenty-seven years. However, his arrest failed to put out the fire[13] which he had ignited in the hearts of the common people. To them, he was a symbol of justice and equality. All through the years while Mandela was in jail, powerful protests continued to rock the country and the ruling government. Everywhere, loud and angry voices demanded the same rights for all. Finally, when Mandela was released from prison on 11 February 1990, the event was broadcast live[14] all over the world. On 27 April 1994, the first free and fair elections were held in South Africa in which every adult citizen of the country was allowed to vote. On 10 May 1994, Nelson Mandela became the first ever black President of South Africa. It had taken more than forty years for his dream - of a democratic and just society where people lived together in harmony - to finally come true.

Even after his retirement[15], Mandela continued to work for the common people. He was an active member of several groups that work for the benefit of the society. He received many awards internationally. Among these were the Bharat Ratna (1990), the Nobel Peace Prize (1993), Freedom of the City given by the city of Johannesburg (1994) and the Honorary Citizenship of Canada (2001).

Mandela died at his home in Johannesburg on 5 December, 2013.

Wordfile

12. **Armed struggle** is fighting with weapons.
13. To **put out the fire** is to stop feelings of anger.
14. If something is **broadcast live**, it is shown on television or aired on the radio as it happens.
15. **Retirement** is the period in someone's life after they stop working, usually because they are old.

Comprehension 1

A Arrange these sentences in the order of the events in the passage.

1. Nelson Mandela became the President of South Africa. ________
2. Mandela was asked to leave university because he disagreed with many of the university's policies. ________
3. He was sent to prison where he spent the next 27 years of his life. ________
4. He moved to Johannesburg where he worked first as a security guard and then as an accountant. ________
5. He became very involved in politics and started fighting for the rights of the common black people. ________
6. He was released from prison in 1990. ________

B Match the first half of the sentences with the second half.

1. In the Afrikaans language, 'apartheid' means	a. life became a lot worse for most black people living in South Africa.
2. Nelson Mandela was born	b. his mother looked after him and made sure he went to school.
3. After Mandela's father died,	c. 'being separate or apart'.
4. Neither of Nelson Mandela's parents went to school	d. on 18 July, 1918, in Umtau in South Africa.
5. After the National Party came to power in 1948,	e. but they made sure that their son received a good education.

C Are the sentences true (T) or false (F)?

1. It was a school teacher who gave Mandela the English name, Nelson. ________
2. Mandela had to stop studying at the university because he could not pay for the course. ________
3. At the start of his struggle for the rights of the common black people, Mandela did not believe in using violence. ________
4. From 1960, the protests became less and less violent. ________
5. Mandela's arrest and imprisonment did not stop the protests. ________
6. Nelson Mandela was called 'Madiba' by many of the people of South Africa. ________

Comprehension 2

1. What kind of person was Nelson Mandela? What adjectives would you use to describe his character? Discuss with your partner and write a brief character sketch.
2. Nelson Mandela's freedom marked one of the most important events in the history of South Africa. Justify the statement with reference to the story.
3. VBQ Mandela and his followers first adopted Gandhi's method of non-violence to protest against apartheid, but later they took up violent means. Do you think Mandela was right in using violence? Do you think anything can be solved through violent means? Discuss and give reasons for your opinion.

Vocabulary check

Match the phrases in column A with their meanings in column B.

A	B
1. to play a key role in something	a. to fight with weapons
2. in favour of something	b. a life of great suffering
3. a living hell	c. to do the same thing as someone else did
4. to take upon yourself	d. to be very important and have a big effect on something
5. to take up arms	e. to take charge of something
6. to follow in someone's footsteps	f. thinking that something is a good idea

Language skills

Pronunciation

When a word is pronounced, it can be broken up into parts.

These parts are called **syllables**.

Each syllable has one vowel sound.

pen (one syllable) *pa·per* (two syllables)

A **Use your dictionary to find out how many syllables there are in these words.**

1. explosion ______
2. democracy ______
3. inequality ______
4. political ______
5. heroic ______
6. position ______
7. discrimination ______
8. society ______

When we pronounce a word, we usually say one syllable with more force than the other syllables.

*protest (verb) = pro·**test*** *involvement = in·**volve**·ment*

In the verb form of *protest*, a two syllable word, we put stress on the second syllable. We can show it as **o O**. In *involvement*, a three-syllable word, we put stress on the second syllable. We show it as **o O o**.

When we say the words *protest* (noun), *after* and *sacrifice*, we stress the first syllable. For two-syllable words (*protest* and *after*), we show the stress as **O o**. For three-syllable words like sacrifice, we show this as **O o o**.

*protest (noun) = **pro**·test* *after = **af**·ter* *sacrifice = **sac**·ri·fice*

B **Read these words aloud. Which syllables are stressed? Put the words in the correct column.**

o O o	O o o
involvement	sacrifice
______	______
______	______
______	______
______	______
______	______
______	______
______	______
______	
______	

~~involvement~~ ~~sacrifice~~
difficult heroic
important beginning
injustice position
policy devoted
successful retirement
explosion benefit
quality citizen
President treasure

Reading 2

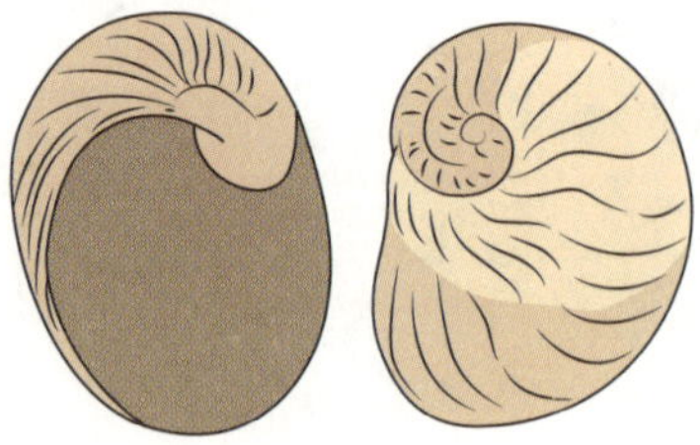

This short story is about a little girl called Val and her grandmother, and their trip to the beach. In the story, you will read about shells with different names. These names relate to the colour or the shape of the shells. Have you seen shells on a beach? Can you identify them?

Note that the story was written by an American author and there are a number of American words and spellings in it.

Baby's Ears

Mom poured herself a glass of orange juice. 'I'm worried about Grandma,' she said. I was pouring syrup on my French toast[1], hot and sweet, just the way I like it.

'Why?' I asked, as I licked a drop of syrup from my fork.

'Well, remember before she moved to Florida, how early Grandma would get up?'

'Before the sun,' I said, 'to make pancakes[2].'

My mom nodded. 'But now Grandma sleeps most of the day or watches television. I can't get her out of the house, and she won't try to make friends.' Mom frowned and lowered her voice. 'Grandma's even talking about going back to New York.'

'Back to New York? But you said that she couldn't live alone any more. That's why she came to live here.' I like Florida. Of course, I have a lot of girlfriends to play with in my sixth-grade class.

'If Grandma went back to New York she would have to live in a nursing home,' my mother told me. 'That's a place where old people live and nurses take care of them.'

'It sounds like a hospital to me,' I said. I thought for a minute. 'I'll find a way to make Grandma like Florida.'

Mom smiled and said, 'I wish you could.'

Wordfile

1. **French toast** is bread that has been dipped in egg and then fried.
2. A **pancake** is a thin, flat, round food made from milk, flour and eggs, cooked in a frying pan.

After school, I saw Grandma watching television and figured she hadn't moved all day. In my room, I sat on my bed and took out my seashell collection. I had found Striped Whelks, Purple Sea Snails and even a Queen Conch Shell. You can hold a conch shell up to your ear and actually hear the ocean waves. My very favorite shell was called a Baby's Ear. It's a beautiful white shell shaped just like the ear of a baby, all swirly[3] and delicate[4].

Looking at my seashells gave me an idea. I went into the living room and sat on the couch. 'Did you ever go to the beach when you were little, Grandma?' I asked.

'Once my mother took me, but I didn't enjoy it at all,' she said, frowning.

'Really?' I took an oatmeal cookie from the plate on the coffee table. 'Why not?'

'I'm afraid of the water and I can't swim.' Grandma pursed her lips[5] as though she'd tasted a lemon. I wished Grandma could feel the way I did about the beach. I loved to see the pelicans[6] flying over the water, and once I even saw a huge iguana[7].

'Well, I was wondering if you could take me to the beach, Grandma. I need some new shells for my collection.'

Grandma didn't even look up from the TV. 'I'm watching my show, Val. Can't you go by yourself?'

'No, I'm not allowed to go to the beach by myself. Please,' I begged, imagining Grandma in a nursing home.

'Oh, all right,' Grandma sighed. She took my hand as we left the house, and we walked to the beach. The sun felt hot enough to melt metal. I handed Grandma a plastic bag. 'Here. This is for the seashells you find.'

'Oh, I'll leave that to you,' she said. A soft ocean breeze blew her grey curls across her eyes.

I shook my head. 'No, Grandma. I need all the help I can get.'

'Oh, all right,' she said. We walked side by side up the beach, our heads down, looking for only the most beautiful shells.

Wordfile

3. **Swirly** describes a pattern of lines that look as if they were made by moving something round and round.
4. If something is **delicate**, you can break it easily because it is very thin.
5. If you **purse** your **lips**, you move them into a small, rounded shape, often showing that you do not like something.
6. A **pelican** is a large bird with a bag of skin under its beak for storing the fish that it catches.
7. An **iguana** is a large, grey-green lizard.

'Doesn't look like there's much to choose from,' Grandma said, shading her eyes with her hand. 'Maybe we should go home.'

'Not yet, Grandma. I'll go ahead like a scout[8] and see if I find anything good.' I looked back at her as I walked ahead. Grandma stood watching the ocean waves and the seagulls that flew over the water searching for fish. She took off her shoes and carried them.

I ran on ahead and slipped a Pink Triton shell from my pocket, dropping it in the sand. Farther up the beach, I did the same with my Blue Starfish and my Green Serpent Star. Finally, I dropped my favorite shell, the Baby's Ear.

Just then, I heard Grandma shout, 'Val! Look what I found!' Grandma stood in the sand, holding up the Pink Triton.

'That's beautiful, Grandma!' I cried. 'It will look great in my collection!'

Grandma nodded and smiled. 'Let's keep looking!' she said, suddenly excited. I pretended to pass right by the Blue Starfish, but Grandma bent down slowly and picked it up. 'Val! Look at this starfish. It's blue.'

'You're really good at this, Grandma!'

She carried her plastic bag proudly. At last, Grandma came to my favorite shell.

'Val, look at this strange thing.' She handed it to me. I cradled the shell in my hand. 'It's called a Baby's Ear because that's what it looks like.'

'You're pretty good at this yourself, Val,' Grandma said, giving me a hug. On the way home, we waded[9] in the ocean. Grandma seemed to have forgotten her fear of water.

We met my mum on the front porch[10]. 'We've been to the beach,' Grandma told her. 'And you know, I think I'll start a shell collection of my own. You can help me, Val.'

'OK, Grandma,' I said.

My mum and I shared a secret smile.

Valerie Allen

Wordfile

8. A **scout** is someone who goes in front of the main group of people in order to look for a particular thing.
9. If you **wade**, you walk through water.
10. A **porch** is a small covered area at the entrance to a house.

Comprehension 1

A Tick [✓] the correct option.

1. At the start of the story, Val is
   a. washing up after breakfast. ☐
   b. preparing her breakfast. ☐
   c. preparing lunch. ☐
2. Val and her family live in
   a. England. ☐
   b. New York. ☐
   c. Florida. ☐
3. Val's mother is worried because her mother
   a. won't leave the house or do anything. ☐
   b. eats very little. ☐
   c. looks ill. ☐
4. Val's grandmother said that she could not take her to the beach because
   a. she was watching a TV show. ☐
   b. she was unwell. ☐
   c. it was raining outside. ☐
5. To make her grandma interested in collecting shells, Val
   a. drops her favourite shells in the sand for her to pick up. ☐
   b. tells her all about shells. ☐
   c. shows her grandma her shell collection. ☐
6. The visit to the beach makes Val's grandma want to
   a. learn to swim. ☐
   b. start collecting shells. ☐
   c. find out more about the wildlife at the beach. ☐

B Answer these questions.

1. What does Val say to her grandma to persuade her to come to the beach?
2. What was the name of Val's favourite shell? Why was it called so?
3. What action shows that by the end of the story, Grandma had forgotten her fear of water?

4. 'I'm afraid of the water and I can't swim.'
   a. Who is the speaker here? Who is she talking to?
   b. What does the listener love about the beach? What had that person seen on the beach once?
   c. What request did the listener make immediately after this?

Comprehension 2

1. What did Val's grandma find on the beach? How did it make her feel?
2. How would you describe Val's character? Use instances from the story to support your answer.
3. (VBQ) By dropping her shells on the beach, Val tricks her grandma into thinking she has found the shells. Tricking people is usually a bad thing. Do you think Val does a bad thing to her grandma? Think about Val's reasons for tricking her in this way and write them down.

Vocabulary

Words in American and British English

A The story 'Baby's Ears' includes some words that are used in American English. Match the American words with words in British English that have the same meaning.

1. mom	a. French fries
2. chips	b. biscuit
3. couch	c. film
4. cookie	d. mum
5. movie	e. sofa
6. apartment	f. holiday
7. vacation	g. flat

B **Complete the sentences with British English words. The corresponding American English words are given in brackets.**

rubber lift holiday garden fringe aubergine bonnet car park football jumper

1. I used a __________ (**eraser**) to rub out the mistakes.
2. Fry the __________ (**eggplant**) in a little oil for five minutes until it is brown.
3. My dad opened the __________ (**hood**) of the car to look at the engine.
4. Is there a __________ (**parking lot**) where we can leave the car?
5. Hey, Mira, you've had your hair cut. I like your __________ (**bangs**)!
6. My dad was in the __________ (**yard**), planting some flowers.
7. We went to the seaside for our __________ (**vacation**).
8. We need to go to the second floor. Shall we take the __________ (**elevator**)?
9. My aunt gave me a __________ **(sweater)** as a Christmas present.
10. Our team has won the inter-school __________ **(soccer)** competition.

Grammar

Simple past and past continuous tenses

Look at the opening lines of the story:

Mom poured herself a glass of orange juice. 'I'm worried about Grandma,' she said. ***I was pouring syrup*** *on my French toast, hot and sweet, just the way I like it.*

Notice the past continuous phrase, *I* ***was*** *pour****ing*** *syrup*. The past continuous is often used in this way in storytelling. It tells you what was happening when the story started. It is not used to tell you the main events of the story. Instead, it is used to describe little details that create the 'world' in which the story happens. The action in the past continuous, (pouring syrup), tells us that Val was enjoying preparing her breakfast when the important conversation about her grandma started. Here are two more examples of the past continuous being used in this way:

The sun ***was shining*** *and the birds* ***were singing*** *as we set off down the street.*

The wind ***was blowing*** *and the leaves* ***were swirling*** *around my feet as I stepped out into the night.*

Notice how the tense changes from the past continuous to the simple past.

A **Complete the sentences with the given verbs. Use the past continuous tense for describing what was happening when an event took place. Use the simple past for the event itself.**

1. Samreen and I [a]__________ (dance) and other people [b]__________ (chat). Suddenly, there [c]__________ (be) a loud crash and the lights [d]__________ (go out).
2. I [a]__________ (relax) with my family. We [b]__________ (watch) television. All of a sudden, we [c]__________ (hear) a loud cry outside the house.
3. I [a]__________ (talk) to Jasbir. She [b]__________ (show) me some photos. We [c]__________ (have) such a nice time. Then I [d]__________ (notice) the time. It was past 10 o'clock!
4. We [a]__________ (enjoy) our picnic and [b]__________ (look) at the beautiful birds when suddenly a crow [c]__________ (swoop) down and [d]__________ (take) our sandwiches.

B **Write a short paragraph describing an event in the same way as in Exercise A. Use the past continuous and the simple past tenses.**

Subject and Predicate

Every sentence has a subject and a predicate. Look at these sentences:

My very favorite shell was called a Baby's Ear.

Grandma didn't even look up from the TV.

In the first sentence, ***My very favorite shell*** is the subject while ***was called a Baby's Ear*** is the predicate. It tells us something about the subject.

In the second sentence, ***Grandma*** is the subject, while ***didn't even look up from the TV*** is the predicate.

The **subject** tells us whom or what the sentence is about. It can be a word or a group of words. The **predicate** tells us something about the subject or the action performed by it in the sentence.

C **Circle the subject and underline the predicate in these sentences.**

1. The naughty child broke the vase.
2. A gaggle of geese flew across in the sky.
3. I study in a boarding school.

4. My cousin participated in a drawing competition.
5. Ravi and Rohit are good friends.
6. Raj is playing chess with his friends.
7. The dolphin jumped out of the water.
8. The wizard took out his wand to fight the monster.

Listening

Making requests

A **Listen to four conversations. For each conversation, say whether the second person agrees to the first person's request. Circle Yes or No.**

1. Yes/No
2. Yes/No
3. Yes/No
4. Yes/No

B **Listen to the conversations again and complete the requests.**

1. Mum, ________ you mind giving Neha and me a lift to Gurjit's house this afternoon?
2. I was ________ if I could borrow that book on whales, please?
3. Could you ________ turn the music down a little, please?
4. Would it be ________ for you to repair my bicycle, Dad?

Speaking

Responding to requests

Notice the way people agree to requests.

Could I possibly borrow that book?

Of course./Sure, no problem./Yes, take it!/Absolutely!

Notice the way people refuse requests. Often, instead of saying *no* and apologizing, people state the reason for which they cannot accept the request. They may also suggest a different plan.

I'm watching my show, Val. Can't you go by yourself?

A **In pairs, take turns to ask your partner *politely* for something. Your partner may say *yes* or *no*. Use the given request suggestions and some helpful phrases to ask for help and to offer/refuse help.**

1. On a train, ask a stranger to open a window that is near them. (You can't reach it.)
2. In a café, ask if you can take a chair that is at someone else's table.
3. Ask your friend's mother if you can have the recipe for a delicious cake that she had made.
4. Ask your friend's father if you can borrow a pen.
5. Ask your friend's mother if you can stay at their house on Friday night.
6. Ask your teacher if she can explain her comments on an English essay that you wrote for homework.

Useful phrases for making requests

Would you mind ...?
Could you/I possibly ...?
I was wondering if you/I could ...?
Would it be possible for you to ...?
Might I ...?

Useful phrases for saying *yes*

Of course ...
I will be glad to ...
I will be delighted ...
Sure, no problem!
Yes, take it!
Absolutely!

Useful phrases for saying *no*

I'm afraid I'm busy ...
I'm afraid I can't ...
I'm cooking dinner/working, etc at the moment.

Writing

Writing a story: descriptive writing

When you write a story, it is important to create an atmosphere. By creating an atmosphere or 'mood' for your story, you will make your reader feel interested and involved. Here are a few tips to help you.

A sense of place

First, try to give the reader a sense of the place where the action happens. Of course, you can do this by describing the appearance of the place. You can also help to create the 'world' that the story is set in by describing one or two details about something that is happening in that place.

Grandma stood watching the ocean waves and the seagulls that flew over the water searching for fish.

Weather

Remember the weather! Weather is very useful for creating atmosphere. For example, sunny weather generally creates a happy atmosphere; storms add a sense of drama and excitement. Descriptions of weather can also add to the sense of the place where the story is happening.

She took my hand as we left the house, and we walked to the beach. The sun felt hot enough to melt metal.

Adjectives

Use adjectives. A few carefully chosen adjectives will give the reader a strong sense of what you are describing. Adjectives may describe things that you can see or things that you can hear. They may also describe things that you can taste, touch or smell.

I was pouring syrup on my French toast, ***hot*** *and* ***sweet****, just the way I like it.*

A In your notebook, write the opening two paragraphs of a story. Try to create an atmosphere, or 'world' for the action to take place, using the tips above.

Describe an interesting event that happened when you were spending your summer vacation at your grandparents' house.

Begin like this:

I always looked forward to summer vacations because this was the time I spent with my grandparents in our home town. But this year, they were even more special ...

Poem

This poem is narrated by a dog who tells us his life story. He starts out on the streets, without an owner or a home, but then something very good happens to him. Read the poem to find out what happens to the dog.

Rescue Poem

Once I was a lonely dog, just looking for a home.
I had no place to go, no one to call my own.
I wandered[1] up and down the streets, in rain, in heat and in snow.
I ate whatever I could find; I was always on the go[2].
My skin would itch, my feet were sore, my body ached with pain.
And no one stopped to give a pat or gently say my name.

I never saw a loving glance[3]; I was always on the run[4].
For people thought that hurting me was really lots of fun.

Then one day I heard a voice so gentle, kind and sweet, and
arms so soft reached down to me and took me off my feet.
'No one again will hurt you,' was whispered in my ear.
'You'll have a home to call your own, where you will know no fear.
'You will be dry, you will be warm, you'll have enough to eat, and rest assured[5] that when you sleep, your dreams will all be sweet.'

I was afraid, I must admit, I've lived so long in fear.
I can't remember when I let a human come so near.
And as she tended[6] to my wounds and bathed and brushed my fur,
She told me 'bout the rescue group and what it meant to her.
She said, 'We are a circle, a line that never ends.
And in the center there is you protected by new friends.'

'And all around you are the ones that check the pounds[7],
And those that share their home after you've been found.
And all the other folk are searching near and far.
To find the perfect home for you, where you can be a star.'
She said, 'There is a family, that's waiting patiently,
and pretty soon we'll find them, just you wait and see.
And then they'll join our circle they'll help to make it grow,
so there'll be room for more like you, who have no place to go.'

Wordfile

1. If you **wander**, you walk around in no particular direction.
2. If you are **on the go**, you are moving all the time.
3. A **glance** is a quick look at something or someone.
4. Someone who is **on the run** is trying to escape from someone else.
5. You say **'rest assured'** to tell someone not to worry because something good will definitely happen.
6. If you **tend to** someone or something, you look after them.
7. A **pound** is a place where rescued street dogs are kept.

I waited very patiently, the days they came and went.
Today's the day I thought, my family will be sent.
Then just when I began to think it wasn't meant to be,
there were people standing there just gazing down at me.
I knew them in a heartbeat[8]; I could tell they felt it too.
They said, 'We have been waiting for a special dog like you.'

Now every night I say a prayer to all the gods that be.
'Thank you for the life I live and all you've given me.
But most of all protect the dogs in the pound and on
the street,
And send a Rescue Person to lift them off their feet.'

Arlene Pace

Wordfile

8. If you do something **in a heartbeat**, you do it very quickly. (A heartbeat is the short, quick beat of your heart in your chest.)

Poetry appreciation

Answer the questions.

1. When the dog was on the streets and without a home, how did people treat him?
2. 'And as she tended to my wounds and bathed and brushed my fur
   she told me 'bout the rescue group and what it meant to her.'
   a. Who is referred to as 'she' in the lines above?
   b. What do the above lines tell you about her?
   c. What does the rescue group do?

3. The person who picks the dog up and takes him home explains that there are three types of people in the rescue group. One group looks in the pounds where the homeless dogs are kept. Another group finds new homes for those dogs. How does the third group help the dogs on the street?
4. Who is the narrator of this poem? How did you feel after reading the poem?
   Do you think you would have felt differently if the poem were narrated by the rescue worker?
5. The poem is very sad to begin with, but ends on a happy note. What happens to the dog after the lady from the rescue group picks him up?
6. The last words in each pair of lines rhyme with each other. (This means that they have the same sound: *home/own, snow/go, pain/name*, etc.) Take turns to read the poem aloud to your partner. Pay attention to these rhyming words.
7. How do you think the poet feels about dogs? What does she think about the way people treat dogs?

Activity

A **In every city, there are government-run hospitals as well as non-government organizations which work for the welfare of animals and birds. Find out about four such organizations in your city. In groups, pay a visit to these organizations to learn about their activities, including the problems they face. For instance, many such organizations do not receive enough funds or lack adequate resources. Then, complete the following table.**

Name of the organization	Facilities offered	Cost	Problems faced by the organization (if any)

Best equipped organization: ____________________

B **Imagine that you are a member of a non-government organization that works for stray animals. Create a poster to raise awareness among school children about the organization's activities.**

Your poster should include the following:

- name of the organization
- a catchy slogan
- activities
- how students can participate and make a difference
- address, contact number, timings

2 Amusing Incidents

In this unit, I will ...

- learn some proverbs
- learn the usage of the hyphen and dash
- learn about phrases and clauses
- role-play informal conversations and have a debate

Warm-up

A **Look at these pictures. They are related to well-known fables and stories. Write down the names of the stories that they are related to, and add a line on the role the cat plays in each.**

1.

____

2.

____

3.

____

B **Work with a partner. Tell your partner about a time when your pet fell ill. Describe how you took care of it, how the illness was treated and how it finally got cured.**

C **Is it healthier to feed pets food that is specially prepared for them? Or, is it acceptable to give them food prepared for humans? Conduct a survey among pet owners in your neighbourhood to find out what they do. Share your findings in class.**

Reading 1

Read about a real-life exchange of letters between a cat owner and a Customer Relations executive of the company from which he buys food for his pet. The exchange began with the owner's letter of complaint when his cat fell ill after eating the pet food. The letters are tongue-in-cheek and often figurative in meaning.

Feline Eating Disorders

Customer Relations Department
Mars Petcare UK
3D Dundee Road
Slough
Berkshire SL 14LG

Dear Customer Relations,

I have a cat called Nahla. She's named after the lioness in *The Lion King*. She doesn't look much like a lion. In fact, she looks like a tiger that shrank[1] in the wash because she's small and stripy[2], but she seems to like the name.

She also likes Catty Foods' 'Meat-o-Jelly'. In fact, she likes it so much that she gets very stroppy[3] when we give her crunchy cat food, which the vet says we have to on account of her gum disease. Her favourite Catty Food is the poultry selection. She doesn't like the 'Fishy Foods' ones – probably because we live a long way from the sea.

Anyway, I am beginning to get a little worried about Nahla because she keeps being sick after she has eaten her Meat-o-Jelly. Unfortunately, she seems to prefer to throw up in the house instead of in other people's gardens. I don't particularly like the look or smell of Meat-o-Jelly when it's

Wordfile

1. If something **shrank**, it reduced in size.
2. If something is **stripy**, it has stripes on its body.
3. If someone is **stroppy**, they are bad-tempered.

fresh from the pouch. When it's been inside a cat for ten minutes, it's not nice at all!

I think she is displaying a lot of the classic symptoms of bulimia[4]. I have looked up bulimia on the NHS[5] website and it says that low self-esteem[6] could be a major factor.

Nahla is much smaller than all the other cats in the neighbourhood and her tummy is a bit 'saggy'[7] since she had kittens when she was very young. I suspect that she is being bullied. She is also adopted, (she was already over a year old when she came to us) so perhaps she is insecure[8].

As you are clearly *very* expert in the area of feline[9] nutrition, I was hoping that you may be able to offer some advice.

Yours hopefully,

Anthony

The following letter is a reply from a Customer Relations executive of Catty Foods.

Order Ref 38911&993

Dear Anthony,

Thanks for getting in touch about our products.

Naturally we are concerned by this and would like to bring it to the attention of our Quality Control Managers. Therefore, if you have retained[10] any pouches from the batch in question, could you please return them to us for examination? We will then be able to respond to your complaint more thoroughly.

You can use the short Freepost address quoted below:

FAO Susan 38986993
Freepost
Catty Foods

Regarding Nahla's other Issues, there are many reasons why cats will vomit, such as eating their favourite food too quickly, eating something odd while out toileting

Wordfile

4. **Bulimia** is an illness in which a person repeatedly eats too much and then forces oneself to vomit.
5. **NHS** stands for National Health Service, the public health service in Britain, which is paid for by taxes.
6. **Self-esteem** is the feeling of being happy with your own character and abilities.
7. If something is **saggy**, it droops or has lost its firmness.
8. If someone is **insecure**, they are not confident about themselves.
9. Something that is **feline** is related to members of the cat family.
10. When you **retain** something, you keep it.

in other people's gardens, or even if they don't particularly like your carpet. Low self-esteem isn't usually a problem for cats. It is usually quite the opposite. So I would rule out bulimia as a cause. It is possible that she is anxious about her adoption. Perhaps you could give her access to your Internet so that she could try to trace her relatives that way instead? Maybe she would like to live closer to the sea: you could always sell up and move to see if that makes a difference (that would also solve her issues with your carpet.)

I look forward to hearing from you. Please quote the above reference number and your postal address when contacting us.

If you need any more help or advice, please don't hesitate to let me know.

Yours sincerely,
Susan Hendy
Consumer Care Team
0800738800

Comprehension 1

A Are the sentences true (T) or false (F)?

1. Anthony has a tiger named Nahla. ____
2. Nahla is happy when she gets crunchy cat food. ____
3. Anthony feels Nahla has the classic symptoms of bulimia. ____
4. Nahla was worried about her adoption. ____
5. Susan advises Anthony to live in the mountains. ____
6. Susan suggested that Nahla should not be given any access to the Internet. ____

B **Answer in brief.**

1. Nahla's favourite Catty Food is: ______________________
2. Susan worked as: ______________________
3. This is the reason for Nahla's insecurity: ______________________
4. Nahla was named after this character: ______________________
5. This is the reason Anthony was worried about Nahla: ______________________

C **Answer in a sentence.**

1. What reason did Anthony give for Nahla not liking 'Fishy Food'?
2. What is the classic symptom of bulimia?
3. What method did Susan suggest to help Nahla find her relatives?
4. What, according to Susan, might help Anthony solve Nahla's problem with his carpet?
5. 'Low self-esteem isn't usually a problem for cats. It is usually quite the opposite.' What do these lines mean?

Comprehension 2

Answer the questions.

1. Do you think that Anthony is overreacting to his pet's illness? Answer with examples from the passage.
2. How is Anthony's letter different from usual complaint letters? Mention two differences.
3. Susan Hendy makes a few suggestions in her letter. Do you think she was joking with Anthony, or was her advice genuine and aimed at helping him?
4. Is it important to spend time with pets? Do you think they feel neglected when we do not give them enough attention? Give reasons for your answer. VBQ

Vocabulary check

A **Fill in the blanks with words from the passage.**

1. Do not spill tea on the ______________ in the room.
2. Rana had not returned home. So, his mother was quite ______________.
3. The ______________ examined the dog and gave it some medicines.

4. The lion is a member of the ______________ family.
5. We must have a balanced diet so that we get proper ______________.

B **Match these proverbs related to cats with their meanings.**

Proverbs	Meanings
1. After dark, all cats are leopards.	a. Being too interested about another person's business may land one in trouble.
2. A cat has nine lives.	b. When the person in charge is absent, people take advantage of the situation to do what they want.
3. Who will bell the cat?	c. A person can take a lot of risks and still come out unharmed.
4. Curiosity killed the cat.	d. Things are not always what they seem.
5. When the cat is away, the mice will play.	e. Who has enough courage to perform a dangerous task?

Language skills

Punctuation: hyphen (-) and dash (–)

Look at these sentences from the text.

I don't particularly like the look or smell of ***Meat-o-Jelly*** *when it's fresh from the pouch.*

Low ***self-esteem*** *isn't usually a problem for cats.*

Both sentences contain words with a hyphen.

The **hyphen (-)** is a punctuation mark that is used:

- in compound words: a *good-looking man*, a *well-known singer*, *a five-year-old boy*
- in numbers: *twenty-one* to *ninety-nine*
- with certain prefixes, such as *self-*, *ex-* and *re-*: *self-respect*, *ex-teacher*, *re-elect*
- in nouns that come from phrasal verbs: *a break-in*, *a build-up*

- to show that a word has spilled over to the next line in a printed book. The word may actually not have a hyphen.

Note: Many compound words (especially compound nouns) which were written with a hyphen in the past are now written as two separate words or, more commonly, as one word. It's always best to refer to a good dictionary when in doubt.

A **dash (–)** is a little longer than a hyphen. It is used:

- for periods of time, in place of 'to': 1780–1850
- to replace a comma, a colon or a semicolon, in order to show (1) emphasis, (2) an interruption or (3) a change of thought

  She doesn't like the 'Fishy Foods' ones – probably because we live a long way from the sea.

Rewrite the sentences, inserting a dash or a hyphen in the appropriate places.

1. You must go to the check in area when you arrive at the airport. (hyphen)
2. The snow covered peaks looked beautiful from a distance. (hyphen)
3. The first time I went for a swimming class, I was terrified I was only three at the time. (dash)
4. Malala Yousafzai's tale is that of a sixteen year old girl fighting for the right to an education. (hyphens)
5. We decided to take a few practical things for our camping trip a torch, a first aid kit and a compass. (dash, hyphen)
6. Fifty five participants from all over the world were chosen for the Antarctic expedition. (hyphen)
7. They told us that the man was an ex soldier. (hyphen)
8. The book was written by Khushwant Singh (1915 2014). (dash)
9. The latest self help book written by this author has become a bestseller. (hyphen)
10. The period when the British ruled over India was 1757 1947. (dash)
11. The scientist he is a Nobel laureate was honoured by the university. (dash)
12. Question number seventy seven is the hardest one in this chapter. (hyphen)

Reading 2

What is the most severe punishment that you have ever received? What were your feelings?

Tom Sawyer is a mischievous boy who lives with his aunt and his half-brother. He misses school and dirties his clothes in a fight. As punishment, his aunt makes him whitewash the fence. Read on to find how he cleverly finds a way out of it.

Characters

Tom: a ten-year-old boy
Jim: a servant at Aunt Polly's house
Ben and **Joe**: friends of Tom
Aunt Polly

Tom Paints the Fence

(The pavement outside the fence of a house. It is morning, and a few boys go by, laughing, shouting, playing tag. Two more boys play leap-frog across the pavement. Tom enters through the gate. He carries a large bucket of whitewash and a broad brush. He sets the bucket down and mournfully[1] looks at the long length of fence. Sighing, he dips his brush and passes it along a section of the topmost plank. He steps back and surveys the insignificant white streak, comparing it to the far-reaching continent of unpainted wood. He sits down sadly on an upturned barrel. Jim comes through the gate, holding an empty pail.)

Tom: Where are you going to, Jim?

Jim: To the pump to fetch the water.

Tom: Say, Jim, I'll fetch the water if you'll whitewash some.

Jim *(shakes his head and takes a step back)*: Can't do it, Master Tom. Miss Polly, she expects you'll ask me to whitewash, and she told me to go along and mind my own business.

(Tom produces a marble from his pocket and shows it to Jim, as if to bribe him. Jim examines the marble.)

Jim: That's a mighty gay marble, I tell you!

Tom: And for you, if you'll just do a little whitewashing while I ...

Jim: But, Master Tom, I am mighty afraid Miss Polly'll ...

Tom: She won't ever know!

About the author

Mark Twain (1835–1910) was the pen name of the American novelist, Samuel L. Clemens. He is one of the best-loved American novelists of all time. *The Adventures of Tom Sawyer*, on which this play is based, and *The Adventures of Huckleberry Finn* are his most popular works.

Wordfile

1. When you do something **mournfully**, you look and feel sad while doing it.

Jim: I'd like to help you, Master Tom, you know that, but ...

Tom: Jim, I'll show you my sore toe!

Jim: Sure 'nuff?

Tom: Sure 'nuff!

(After a second's hesitation, Jim sets down his pail. He collects the marble from Tom and bends over the sore toe, his eyes wide with interest, as Tom begins to unwind the bandage. Aunt Polly's arm, clutching a slipper, descends, giving Jim a beating. Jim grabs his pail with a startled shriek[2] and exits quickly, while Tom leaps to the fence and begins whitewashing energetically.

Aunt Polly leaves. In the distance is heard the long-drawn blast of the Big Missouri[3] *whistle. Tom's eyes widen and he looks longingly in the direction of the sound. The whistle is repeated.*

Ben Rogers, a stout, young man of Tom's age, approaches. He is eating an apple and imitating the sounds and movements of a steamboat as he walks along the pavement.)

Ben: Stop her, Sir! Ting-a-ling-ling! Ship up to back! Tinga-ling-ling! Set her back on the stab board! Ting-a-ling-ling! Chow! Ch-chow-wow!!

(Tom looks down at Ben, then he looks at his brush, and from there, to the fence. An idea seems to be forming in his mind. Quickly, he dips the brush, and turns to the unpainted boards, starting to work determinedly.)

Ben: Come out with your spring line[4]—what're you about there? Take a turn 'round that stump, with the bight[5] of it! Stand by the stage, now let her go! Done with the engines, Sir! Tinng-a-ling-ling!
(*He catches sight of Tom.*) Hi!

(Tom doesn't hear. He surveys[6] his last touch with the eye of an artist, then gives his brush another gentle sweep and surveys the result. Ben ranges[7] up alongside of him, chewing on his apple.)

Hey, you gotta work, hey?

Wordfile

2. When you **shriek**, you make a high-pitched noise, especially to express terror or pain.
3. ***Big Missouri*** was one of the largest steamboats that sailed on the Mississippi river.
4. A **spring line** is a thick rope that is laid diagonally from a ship's front to its end and attached to a fixed point.
5. A **bight** is a curve along the course of a river.
6. When you **survey** something, you look at it closely.
7. When you **range up** to someone, you go near that person.

Tom *(turning, surprised)*: Why, it's you, Ben! I didn't notice.

Ben: Say, I'm going swimming, till Big Mo pulls in. Don't you wish you could come along with us?

(He takes another bite out of his apple. Tom stares at the apple, then forces his eyes away.)

Tom *(carelessly)***:** What do you call work? Whitewashing this fence? It suits Tom Sawyer.

(He resumes his whitewashing. Ben watches for a moment, puzzled.)

Ben: You mean to say you like it?

Tom: I don't see why not. Does a boy get a chance to whitewash a fence every day?

(Ben stops nibbling his apple to consider this remark. Tom sweeps his brush daintily[8] back and forth, steps back to note the effect, adds a touch here and there. Ben watches, absorbed.)

Ben: Say, Tom ... Let me whitewash a little.

Tom *(shaking his head)***:** No, no it wouldn't be right, Ben. You see, Aunt Polly's awfully particular about this fence. It's got to be done very carefully; I reckon[9] there isn't one boy in a thousand, maybe two thousand, that can do it the way it's got to be done.

Ben: Oh, come on now, Tom, let me just try. Say, I'll give you the core of my apple! *(Desperately)* Alright, I'll give you all of it!

(Acting as if he didn't want to, Tom gives up the brush and takes the half-eaten apple. Ben starts to whitewash. Tom sits on the upturned barrel and takes a luxurious bite from the apple.)

Tom: Now, be careful, Ben. I'm risking an awful lot just letting you do that.

Ben: I'll be careful, Tom. I'll do it just like I saw you doing it. *(He makes a stroke.)* Lord almighty, watching that old Missouri come in isn't beans compared to this!

(Once more, in the distance, the Big Missouri *sounds its whistle. Tom looks up anxiously. Ben doesn't even notice. Soon Joe Harper races in, carrying a kite.)*

Wordfile

8. To do something **daintily** is to do it with great care.
9. To **reckon** means to believe.

Joe: Say, Tom, you hear Big Mo? She's rounding Potter's landing. Suppose we cut across the hill, and follow her up along the shore?

Tom: Some other time, Joe. Me 'n Ben's got more important things to do than watching steamboats.

Joe *(puzzled)*: What are you doing that's so important?

Tom: Whitewashing.

Joe: Whitewashing? What do you want to do that for on a Saturday?

Ben *(proudly)*: When else can you get a chance to whitewash a fence?

Joe: Who wants to whitewash a fence?

Tom: That's all you know, Joe Harper. You ever whitewash one?

Joe: No. What's so special about it? *(looking from Ben to Tom)* How come Ben's whitewashing your fence for you? You paying him?

Tom: Paying him? Why, Joe, he begged me so hard I just had to let him for a while. I don't even know that I should have done it. Even for the apple he gave me. Not everybody can whitewash a fence.

Joe: I can whitewash a fence as good as Ben can!

Tom: Well, I don't know. Besides, I just told Ben he could do it awhile. I can't turn around and take the brush away from him, can I?

Joe: I could run home and get a brush. Papa's got one.

Tom: I'm not sure you could do it like it ought to be done.

Joe: Tom, I'll give you my kite!

Tom: Well ...

(Joe hands him his kite. Tom is now sitting on the barrel, holding the kite. Joe and Ben stand side by side whitewashing the fence. Big Mo sounds again. Tom looks

Wordfile

10. A **stopper** is an object, usually made of glass or cork, used to close the lid of a bottle.
11. A **decanter** is a glass container.
12. To have a **lick** at something is to get a chance to work on it.

anxiously at the still largely unpainted fence and looks around. Another boy of Tom's age and size comes down the pavement, swinging a dead rat by a string. Soon, a crowd of boys come along. Besides the kite and the dead rat, the barrel soon holds a window sash, six marbles, a piece of chalk, a glass stopper[10] from a decanter[11], a tin soldier, a couple of tadpoles, six fire crackers, a kitten with one eye, a brass door knob, a dog collar, a knife handle.

In addition to Joe and Ben, an army of boys are gathered around the fence, whitewashing. Tom leans against the barrel, idly watching the working, sweating group.)

Tom: All right, Joe, Billy, Johnny, that's enough. *(Through their chorus of protests)* Sam, Jonah, Chuck, your turn.

Ben: Isn't it time for me again, Tom? There's only one more board left!

(The other boys gather around, demanding a chance at the final board.)

Tom: Now, hold on there, all of you! I'll be fair about it. You can all have a lick[12] at the last board. Just line up, and each of you take one stroke at it. But no cheating!

Joe: First!

(He leaps to the unpainted board, and stands in front of it. Shouting and pushing, the other boys line up behind him. Tom hands the brush to Joe.)

Tom: Only one lick, Joe! Then pass it along.

(In the kitchen. Aunt Polly rises from her knitting.)

Aunt Polly *(muttering to herself)*: I think I'd best get out there and see how much the child did afore running away. I suppose if he's done one quarter of it, I ought to be satisfied. *(She goes out through the kitchen door.)*

(On the pavement, Tom is sitting on the barrel, arranging his wealth. The boys have gone. Aunt Polly comes through the gate, sees Tom, and descends on him.)

Aunt Polly: Is this the way you whitewash a fence, playin' with geegaws[13]? (*She is about to hit him.*)

Tom: But it's all done, Auntie!

Aunt Polly: Tom, don't lie to me — I can't bear it. You haven't been out here long enough to do half of it. *(She turns to look at the fence as she talks, and is dumbfounded[14].)* Well, tell me if it isn't! You can work when you've a mind. *(Suspiciously)* How come you managed to do it so fast?

Tom: Why, Auntie, I just worked away at it, 'thout stoppin'. Just like you told me to.

Aunt Polly: I'm almost ready to believe you're telling me the truth for once. Come in and I'll give you a doughnut. I think you're due for a little treat, and just see how much better it'll taste when you know you've earned it through virtuous[15] effort. *(She goes into the kitchen.)*

(Off stage, Big Mo whistles again, very near.)

(Curtain)

Wordfile

13. A **geegaw** is a showy object of no real value.
14. If you are **dumbfounded**, then you are too surprised to talk.
15. If an action is said to be **virtuous**, then it is believed to have been done with honesty.

Comprehension 1

A **Circle the correct option.**

1. Ben Rogers was eating
   a. a banana. b. an apple. c. a peach.
2. Tom had to whitewash
   a. the fence. b. the house. c. the doors and windows.
3. Jim was carrying an empty pail because
   a. he was going to help Tom.
   b. he was going to the pump to fetch water.
   c. he was going to milk the cow.

4. Tom would not let Ben whitewash the fence because
   a. he wanted to do the work himself.
   b. Aunt Polly was very particular about the work.
   c. he wanted Jim to do the work.
5. Aunt Polly rewarded Tom with
   a. a new bat. b. a doughnut.
   c. the chance to go swimming.

B Answer the questions.

1. 'I'll show you my sore toe!'
   a. Who said these words and to whom?
   b. Why did the speaker say these words?
   c. What did the person spoken to reply?
2. Mention all the treasures Tom collected from his friends.
3. Was Aunt Polly happy with Tom? Give reasons for your answer.

Comprehension 2

Answer these questions.

1. What do you think Tom wanted to do on a Saturday?
2. What was Tom's plan? Explain how he carried it out successfully.
3. Do you think the play is funny? Give examples to support your answer.

VBQ 4. Do you think Tom was right to trick others into doing his work for him? What would you have done if you were in his place?

Vocabulary

A Fill in the blanks using the antonyms of the given words. The antonyms are from the play.

1. When the teacher entered the class, she saw all the students ________________ loudly. (crying)
2. The street behind my school is quite ________________. (narrow)
3. We must cross a busy road ________________. (carelessly)

4. We must always ______________ in following the right path. (disbelieve)
5. My uncle's hair is white, but he is quite ______________. (old)
6. Aunt Polly spoke to Tom ______________. (harshly)
7. The ______________ boy lifted the heavy bag easily. (thin)

B Rearrange the letters to form meaningful words using the given clues.

1. to begin again after an interval: ______________ (merseu)
2. copying someone, usually for comic effect: ______________ (titmiaign)
3. a long, thin line or mark: ______________ (eatsrk)
4. a narrow strip of material used to cover a wound: ______________ (gabdena)
5. to move or come down: ______________ (eesncdd)
6. something unimportant: ______________ (nisigifitnac)
7. something that has a high moral standard ______________ (uiorvstu)
8. to think something or have an opinion about something ______________ (cenkro)

Grammar

Phrases and clauses

A **phrase** is a group of words that forms a part of a sentence but does not make complete sense by itself. It does not have a subject or a verb.

> ***After a second's hesitation***, *Jim sets down his pail.*
> *The book is lying* ***on the table***.

In these two sentences, *after a second's hesitation* and *on the table* are phrases.

A **clause** is a group of words that forms part of a sentence, has a subject and a finite verb. A clause may or may not make complete sense by itself.

> ***Tom leans against the barrel***, *idly watching the working, sweating group.*
> ***When the bell rang***, *the students had to submit the answer scripts.*

In the first sentence, the clause *Tom leans against the barrel* makes complete sense. However, in the second sentence, the clause *When the bell rang* does not make complete sense. It depends on the clause *the students had to submit the answer scripts* to complete its meaning.

A In each sentence, identify whether the words in bold form a phrase or a clause.

1. Sara has all the degrees needed to teach **in a school**.
2. **The new doctor** has been working long hours.
3. **Many people were walking on the beach** even though it was raining heavily.
4. The summer camp was held **on the banks of the river.**
5. The mountaineers were walking carefully as **the rocks under their feet were slippery**.
6. My father drinks a cup of tea **in the morning**.
7. **When the clock struck one**, the mouse ran down the clock.
8. **Across the meadow** lies a beautiful farm.

B Use the correct set of words to complete each sentence. Then, mention if the words form a phrase or a clause.

he has worked very hard	in the morning	the day before he left
after the injury	I do not know the answer	at the station
the computer is not working	who wrote *Kim*	

1. I must write a letter to my father ____________________
2. ____________________ as the topic is not in the syllabus
3. I decided to meet my friend ____________________
4. My uncle's book shop is located ____________________
5. We must call the mechanic because ____________________
6. ____________________, and is successful today.
7. The player had to undergo surgery ____________________
8. Do you know ____________________

Listening

A Listen to the autobiography of a tree and answer the questions.

1. Mention two adjectives used to describe the tree.
2. Who planted the tree and where?
3. What tree is it?

4. Why does the tree have an interesting life?
5. What makes the tree happy?

Arguments

B Listen to the given dialogue. Two brothers, Vijayan and Keerthi, are having an argument. Fill in the gaps.

Vijayan: Hey, what do you think you're doing?

Keerthi: What does it look like? I'm getting some [1]____________ because I'm starving.

Vijayan: You can't eat those [2]____________! They're for the [3]____________ tonight!

Keerthi: I know that!

Vijayan: Well, why did you help yourself to them, then? You know [4]____________ has spent all day baking. I mean, if we all just helped ourselves to the party food, there would be none left by the time the [5]____________ arrived!

Keerthi: Actually, I took one [6]____________ cake. Is that such a big [7]____________?

Vijayan: Well, if we all took a cake each, that would be a problem, [8]____________. I think you'd [9]____________ put that cake back.

Keerthi: Okay, I'll put the cake back if it makes you [10]____________.

Vijayan: Good!

Keerthi: I guess there's other food in the [11]____________ that I can take.

Speaking

A Work in pairs and enact the following situations.

1. The Green Club in your school wants you to make a collage for an upcoming exhibition. But you want to go and watch a play with your friends. You think of asking another member of the club to make the collage instead, saying that you are unwell. But you know that it is wrong to lie. You also realise that she or he is already working very hard for the exhibition, and decide to cancel the play and make the collage yourself.
2. You look in your classmate's English book and notice that the essay that she or he has written is an exact copy of an essay you have read in a book. You have to decide whether to ask your classmate to change the essay, or to tell the teacher about it.

B **With the class divided into two groups, have a group discussion on the topic, 'Should students have more free time to do what they want?' Each group can speak either for or against the motion for five minutes.**

Once the discussion is over, pick out two important points from each group's argument and create a presentation based on them.

Writing

Describing an experience

Write a description of an incident when you were scolded or made fun of in front of a lot of people.

You can use these points in your description:

- where the incident took place
- what you were doing at the time
- how you felt: whether you were embarrassed or angry
- why it was embarrassing
- how the situation was resolved

Useful verbs and phrases

broke/misplaced something
He/She was angry/annoyed/upset with me
Though I admitted that it was my fault ...
I explained that ...
I apologized for ...
It was only sorted out when ...
I didn't realize that...
To make matters worse, ...
What is worse, ...
Unfortunately, ...

Poem

This humorous poem is narrated by a student sitting in an examination hall. However, he cannot write any of the answers because he did not study. Read the poem to find out what he does instead.

Dear Mr Examiner

Thank you so much for your questions
I've read them most carefully through
But there isn't a single one of them
That I know the answer to.

I've written my name as instructed
Put the year, the month and the day
But after I'd finished doing that
I had nothing further to say.

So I thought I'd write you a letter
Fairly informally
About what I can see from my desk here
And what it's like to be me.

Mandy has written ten pages
But it's probably frightful guff[1]
And Angela Smythe is copying
The answers off her cuff.[2]

Miss Quinlan is marking our homework
The clock keeps ticking away
I suppose for anyone outside
It's just another day.

There'll be mothers going on errands[3]
Grandmothers sipping tea
Unemployed men doing crosswords
or watching 'Crown Court' on TV.

The rain has finally stopped here
The sun has started to shine
And in a back garden in Sefton Drive
A housewife hangs shirts on a line.

A class files past to play tennis
The cathedral clock has just pealed[4]

Wordfile

1. **Guff** refers to foolish or silly ideas.
2. The **cuff** is the end part of the sleeve of a shirt.
3. When you run an **errand**, you deliver or collect something on someone else's behalf.
4. To **peal** means to ring loudly.

Wordfile

5. When your face is a **mask**, it has no expression and it is difficult to tell what you are thinking.

A mower chugs backwards and forwards
Up on the hockey field.

Miss Quinlan's just read what I've written
Her face is an absolute mask[5]
Before she collects the papers in
I've a sort of favour to ask.

I thought your questions were lovely
I've only myself to blame
But couldn't you give me some marks
For writing the date and my name?

Gareth Owen

About the poet

Gareth Owen (1936–2002) has written several plays and poems for children. He often presents commonplace activities in a child's everyday life like a special event. 'Salford Road', 'Song of the City' and *The Man with Eyes Like Windows* are some of his other writings for children.

Poetry appreciation

Answer the questions.

1. What were the things that the narrator did before he started writing the poem?
2. What were Mandy and Angela Smythe doing during the exam?
3. What were the adults doing at that time?
4. What are some of the sounds the narrator hears while sitting in the class?
5. The poet said that Miss Quinlan's face was 'an absolute mask'. Explain the meaning of the line. Why do you think her face was a mask?
6. Who is the narrator? What favour does he ask from the examiner?
7. VBQ Neither the narrator nor Angela Smythe knew the answer to the questions. While she copied the answers from her cuff, he wrote a letter. Who, according to you, did the better thing? If you were in a similar situation as the narrator, what would you have done?

Activity

Acrostic poem

An acrostic poem is one in which the first letter of each line together spell out a word or phrase.

Here is an example of an acrostic poem.

Ice Cream

I like all flavours.
Chocolate Excess.
English Toffee.

Cream and Cookies.
Raspberry Delight.
Even Vanilla and
Almond Fudge.

Mouthwatering.

You can write an acrostic poem by following these steps:

1. Choose a word and write it vertically.
2. Select words or phrases that describe your idea.
3. Place those words or phrases on the lines that begin with the same letters.
4. Fill in the rest of the lines to create a poem.

Work with a partner and write an acrostic poem with the word *teacher*.

T ______________________________
E ______________________________
A ______________________________
C ______________________________
H ______________________________
E ______________________________
R ______________________________

3 The Environment

In this unit, I will ...

- use my dictionary to learn more about wild animals
- learn how to use phrasal verbs with and without an object
- learn compound words and words for ways in which animals move
- listen to a passage on preserving the environment and learn how to agree or disagree with someone

Warm-up

A Using the picture clues, find eight words in the word grid that are connected with the natural world.

T	R	G	M	E	U	I	Z	U	G
T	Z	B	M	H	R	X	U	M	K
K	A	N	I	M	A	L	C	D	Q
S	H	K	R	C	I	U	G	E	T
J	G	P	L	A	N	E	T	S	S
U	L	M	J	L	F	L	Q	E	A
N	R	P	B	G	O	V	S	R	D
G	H	R	B	Y	R	Y	U	T	S
L	O	D	E	F	E	S	N	T	O
E	K	Q	R	P	S	K	R	O	I
S	J	W	W	A	T	E	R	V	L

B **Work with a partner. Think of three things that are harmful to the environment and three things we can do to protect the environment.**

1. ______________	1. ______________
2. ______________	2. ______________
3. ______________	3. ______________

Reading 1

The following is the speech that a Canadian girl called Severn Suzuki gave to the participants at the 1992 Earth Summit.

The Earth Summit was an important conference which took place in Rio, Brazil. The aim of the conference was to bring countries together to ensure that economic development would not endanger our planet.

Severn was twelve years old at the time.

Save Our World

Hello, I'm Severn Suzuki speaking for E.C.O. The Environmental Children's Organization.

We are a group of twelve- and thirteen-year-olds trying to make a difference: Vanessa Suttie, Morgan Geisler, Michelle Quigg and me. We raised all the money to come here ourselves, to come 5,000 miles to tell you adults you must change your ways. Coming up here today, I have no hidden agenda[1]. I am fighting for my future.

Losing my future is not like losing an election or a few points on the stock market. I am here to speak for all generations[2] to come.

I am here to speak on behalf of the starving children around the world whose cries go unheard.

I am here to speak for the countless animals dying across this planet because they have nowhere left to go.

I am afraid to go out in the sun now because of the holes in our ozone. I am afraid to breathe the air because I don't know what chemicals are in it.

Wordfile

1. A **hidden agenda** is a secret reason for doing something.
2. A **generation** is a group of people who are about the same age.

I used to go fishing in Vancouver, my home, with my dad, until just a few years ago, we found the fish full of cancers. And now we hear of animals and plants going extinct every day - vanishing forever.

In my life, I have dreamt of seeing the great herds of wild animals, jungles and rainforests full of birds and butterflies, but now I wonder if they will even exist for my children to see.

Did you have to worry about these things when you were my age?

All this is happening before our eyes and yet we act as if we have all the time we want and all the solutions. I'm only a child and I don't have all the solutions, but I want you to realize, neither do you!

You don't know how to fix the holes in our ozone layer.

You don't know how to bring the salmon back up a dead stream.

You don't know how to bring back an animal now extinct.

And you can't bring back the forests that once grew where there is now desert.

If you don't know how to fix it, please stop breaking it!

Here, you may be delegates[3] of your governments, business people, organizers, reporters or politicians - but really you are mothers and fathers, sisters and brothers, aunts and uncles - and all of you are someone's child.

I'm only a child yet I know we are all part of a family, five billion strong, in fact, 30 million species[4] strong - and borders and governments will never change that.

I'm only a child yet I know we are all in this together and should act as one single world towards one single goal.

Wordfile

3. A **delegate** is a person who represents his or her organization at a conference.
4. A **species** is a group of animals, plants or insects that are related.

In my anger, I am not blind, and in my fear, I am not afraid of telling the world how I feel.

In my country, we make so much waste; we buy and throw away, buy and throw away, and yet northern countries will not share with the needy. Even when we have more than enough, we are afraid to share; we are afraid to let go of some of our wealth.

In Canada, we live the privileged[5] life, with plenty of food, water and shelter[6] – we have watches, bicycles, computers and television sets. The list could go on for two days.

Two days ago here in Brazil, we were shocked when we spent time with some children living on the streets. This is what one child told us: 'I wish I were rich and if I were, I would give all the street children food, clothes, medicine, shelter, and love and affection.'

If a child on the street who has nothing is willing to share, why are we, who have everything, still so greedy?

I can't stop thinking that these are children my own age, that it makes a tremendous difference where you are born, that I could be one of those children living in the favellas of Rio; I could be a child starving in Somalia or a victim of war in the Middle East or a beggar in India.

I am only a child yet I know that if all the money spent on war was spent on finding environmental answers, ending poverty and finding treaties, what a wonderful place this earth would be!

At school, even in kindergarten, you teach us how to behave in the world. You teach us:

- not to fight with others
- to work things out
- to respect others
- to clean up our mess
- not to hurt other creatures
- to share – not be greedy

Then why do you go out and do the things you tell us not to do?

Did you know?

Every day, we lose an area of rainforest that is larger than the area of New York City. With that loss of rainforest, experts estimate that 137 species of plants, animals and insects become extinct every day, or about 50,000 species become extinct each year.

Wordfile

5. If you are **privileged**, you have rights or advantages that other people do not have.
6. **Shelter** provides protection from the weather or danger.

Do not forget why you're attending these conferences, who you're doing this for – we are your own children. You are deciding what kind of world we will grow up in. Parents should be able to comfort their children by saying 'everything's going to be all right', 'it's not the end of the world' and 'we're doing the best we can'.

But I don't think you can say that to us any more. Are we even on your list of priorities[7]? My dad always says, 'You are what you do, not what you say.'

Well, what you do makes me cry at night. You grown-ups say you love us. But I challenge you: please make your actions reflect your words. Thank you.

Severn Suzuki

Wordfile

7. A **priority** is a person or thing that is important and requires attention.

Comprehension 1

A Circle the correct option.

1. Severn Suzuki went to Brazil
   a. to participate in an election.
   b. to talk to world leaders.
   c. to visit a rainforest.
2. Severn feels that the adults in the audience
   a. need to admit they don't know how to fix the environment.
   b. need to visit the rainforests before they disappear.
   c. need to continue acting in the same way.
3. From the speech, we can understand that a favella is a place where
   a. many poor people live.
   b. many people die because of war.
   c. people have a lot to share.

4. Severn challenges the adults in the audience
   a. to behave like kindergarteners.
   b. to follow the rules they teach children.
   c. to make children feel more comfortable.

B Are the sentences true (T) or false (F)?

1. Severn Suzuki had to raise $5,000 to go to the Earth Summit. ______
2. Severn stopped fishing with her father because the fish were sick. ______
3. Severn thinks we have plenty of time to find solutions to our environmental problems. ______
4. Severn lives in North America. ______
5. In 1992, the population of the Earth was five billion. ______
6. Severn thinks governments spend too much money on war. ______

Comprehension 2

1. Severn Suzuki gave her speech at the Earth Summit in 1992 – more than 20 years ago. If you had to write a letter to Severn in response to her speech, what would you tell her about the environmental problems we face today?
2. Human beings need to understand that the world does not belong to them alone. Do you agree with the statement? Give reasons for your answer. VBQ

Vocabulary check

A Rearrange the letters to form meaningful words from the speech. Then, complete the sentences using the words.

1. We shouldn't have a __________. We need to say what we mean. (dhined danega)
2. Sadly, much of the air we breathe has __________ in it. (clacimshe)
3. Do you know how many __________ children there are in the world? (gravints)
4. Proper food, water and __________ are things that all people need. (thelers)
5. __________ need to do more to help people in need. (clapitoisnı)
6. He lives on the street and he is a __________ of poverty. (mivitc)
7. Damaging the environment today will put great pressure on future __________ (eeaoignrtns)

B **You came across compound words like *countless*, *forever*, *everything* in the passage. Choose the correct option to form compound words.**

1. white ________

   a. way   b. wash   c. wait

2. pass ________

   a. print   b. pen   c. port

3. life ________

   a. long   b. land   c. light

4. water ________

   a. fall   b. fan   c. frame

5. key ________

   a. chair   b. chest   c. board

6. day ________

   a. bird   b. break   c. beak

7. mail ________

   a. stamp   b. box   c. cargo

8. post ________

   a. office   b. address   c. envelope

Language skills

Dictionary work

Use your dictionary to answer these questions.

1. Describe a hyena.
2. What type of animal is a warthog?
3. Is an impala a bird or a mammal?
4. How is a cheetah different from a leopard?
5. Which is the correct spelling: **wildebeest** or **wilderbeast**?
6. The word 'pride' means 'a feeling of respect for yourself'. Can you find another meaning for the word?
7. What is interesting about the word 'cattle'?
8. Find the word 'baboon'. Is the stress on the first or the second syllable?

Reading 2

You are going to read a passage from Michael Morpurgo's novel, *The Butterfly Lion*. The main character in this novel is a boy called Bertie. At this point in the novel, Bertie is about six and he lives in Africa with his mother and father.

While you are reading, try to decide which of the following animals Bertie saw that he had never seen before:

a male lion	☐
a female lion	☐
a white baby lion	☐

The Butterfly Lion

There was a waterhole[1] downhill from the farmhouse, and some distance away. That waterhole, when there was water in it, became Bertie's whole world. He would spend hours in the dusty compound[2], his hands gripping the fence, looking out at the wonders of the veld[3], at the giraffes drinking, spread-legged, at the waterhole; at the browsing[4] impala, tails twitching, alert; at the warthogs snorting and snuffling under the shade of the shingayi trees; at the baboons, the zebras, the wildebeests, and the elephants bathing in the mud.

But the moment Bertie always longed for was when a pride of lions came padding out of the veld. The impala were the first to spring away, then the zebra would panic and gallop off. Within seconds the lions would have the waterhole to themselves, and they would crouch to drink.

From the safe haven[5] of the compound Bertie looked and learned as he grew up. By now, he could climb the tree by the farmhouse, and sit high in its branches. He could see better from up there. He would wait for his lions for hours on end. He got to know the life of the waterhole so well that he could feel the lions were out there, even before he saw them.

Bertie had no friends to play with, but he always said he was never lonely as a child. At night, he loved reading his books and losing himself in the stories, and by day

About the author

Michael Morpurgo (b. 1943), is a famous English author. He writes novels, poems and plays for the theatre and is best known for his children's stories. His novels frequently combine the topics of friendship and nature. Animals are very important in his writing. His main characters often have special relationships with them.

Wordfile

1. A **waterhole** is a pool of water where animals drink.
2. A **compound** is a group of buildings surrounded by walls.
3. **Veld** is an African word for a flat area of land covered in grass.
4. When an animal **browses**, it feeds on plants.
5. A **safe haven** is a place where you are protected from danger.

Wordfile

6. If you **yearn** to be in a place, you want to be there very much.
7. A **sentinel** is a soldier who guards a building.
8. **Kopje** is an African word for a small rocky hill on the veld.
9. A **larder** is a place where food is kept.
10. If you are **agog**, you are very excited and you want to know more.
11. A **solitary** person or thing is one person or thing, alone.
12. **Gloom** is darkness.
13. **Dusk** is the time of day when it is starting to get dark.

his heart was out in the veld with the animals. That was where he yearned[6] to be. Whenever his mother was well enough, he would beg her to take him outside the compound, but her answer was always the same.

'I can't, Bertie. Your father has forbidden it,' she'd say. And that was that.

The men would come home with their stories of the veld, of the family of cheetahs sitting like sentinels[7] on their kopje[8], of the leopard they had spotted high in his tree larder[9] watching over his kill, of the hyenas they had driven off, of the herd of elephants which had stampeded the cattle. And Bertie would listen wide-eyed, agog[10]. Again and again he asked his father if he could go with him to help guard the cattle. His father just laughed, patted his head, and said it was man's work. He did teach Bertie how to ride, and how to shoot too, but always within the confines of the compound.

Week in, week out, Bertie had to stay behind his fence. He made up his mind, though, that if no one would take him out into the veld, then one day he would go by himself. But something always held him back. Perhaps it was one of those tales he'd been told of black mamba snakes whose bite would kill you within ten minutes, of hyenas whose jaws would crunch you to bits, of vultures who would finish off anything that was left so that no one would ever find even the bits. For the time being he stayed behind the fence. But the more he grew up, the more his compound became a prison to him.

One evening – Bertie must have been about six years old by now – he was sitting high up in the branches of his tree, hoping against hope the lions might come down for their sunset drink as they often did. He was thinking of giving up, for it would soon be too dark to see much now, when he saw a solitary[11] lioness come down to the waterhole. Then he saw that she was not alone. Behind her, and on unsteady legs, came what looked like a lion cub – but it was white, glowing white in the gathering gloom[12] of dusk[13].

While the lioness drank, the cub played at catching her tail; and then, when she had had her fill, the two of them slipped away into the long grass and were gone.

Bertie ran inside, screaming with excitement. He had to tell someone, anyone. He found his father working at his desk. 'Impossible,' said his father. 'You're seeing things that aren't there, or you're telling fibs[14] – one of the two.'

'I saw him. I promise,' Bertie insisted. But his father would have none of it, and sent him to his room for arguing.

His mother came to see him later. 'Anyone can make a mistake, Bertie dear,' she said.

'It must have been the sunset. It plays tricks with your eyes[15] sometimes. There's no such thing as a white lion.'

The next evening Bertie watched again at the fence, but the white lion cub and the lioness did not come, nor did they the next evening, nor the next. Bertie began to think he must have been dreaming it.

A week or more passed, and there had been only a few zebras and wildebeest down at the waterhole. Bertie was already upstairs in his bed when he heard his father riding into the compound, and then the stamp of his heavy boots on the veranda.

'We got her! We got her!' he was saying. 'Huge lioness, massive she was. She's taken half a dozen of my best cattle in the last two weeks. Well, she won't be taking any more.'

Bertie's heart stopped. In that one terrible moment he knew which lioness his father was talking about. There could be no doubt about it. His white lion cub had been orphaned[16].

Michael Morpurgo

Wordfile

14. **Fib** is an informal word for a lie; something you say that you know is not true.
15. If something **plays tricks with your eyes**, it makes you think you can see things which are not really there.
16. If a child or an animal **is orphaned**, both of its parents have died.

Comprehension 1

A Complete the sentences.

1. As a child, Bertie would ________________
2. The moment Bertie always longed for ________________
3. Bertie was not allowed to step out of the compound because ________________
4. One day Bertie spotted ________________
5. The lioness had taken ________________

B Use your imagination to decide who might have made these statements. Write 'Bertie', 'Bertie's mother' or 'Bertie's father'.

1. 'Please, take me outside the compound!' ________________
2. 'Sorry, darling; your father would be very angry with me if I let you go outside.' ________________
3. 'Please, can I help you guard the cattle?' ________________
4. 'No, that's not suitable work for a boy.' ________________
5. 'How dare you argue with me! Go to your room, boy!' ________________
6. 'It's not your fault – it was probably a trick of the light.' ________________

C Read this quote from the first paragraph of this passage:

'That waterhole, when there was water in it, became Bertie's whole world.'

Why do you think the waterhole became Bertie's whole world?

Comprehension 2

A Bertie watched the animals every day from his compound. Do you think he was only fascinated by them or did he long to be as free as them? Give reasons for your answer.

B What do you think happens next in the story?

1. Will Bertie escape from the compound?
2. Will he ever see the white cub?

3. Will the cub survive?
4. How do you think Bertie feels towards his father when he hears the news that the lioness has been killed?
5. Do you think that this news will make Bertie decide to do anything?
6. What sort of man do you think Bertie will be when he grows up?

C Animals hunt because they have to; humans hunt because they can. Do you agree with the statement? Give reasons. VBQ

D In the story, Bertie's father refused to believe that he had seen a white lion. Do you think grown-ups are right to disbelieve something just because a child has said it? VBQ

Vocabulary

A How do these animals move? Circle the correct option.

1. How do rabbits move?
   a. They gallop.
   b. They swim.
   c. They hop.
2. How do birds move?
   a. They soar.
   b. They crawl.
   c. They leap.
3. How do fish move?
   a. They creep.
   b. They climb.
   c. They swim.
4. How do insects move?
   a. They hover.
   b. They trot.
   c. They charge.
5. How do snakes move?
   a. They run.
   b. They slither.
   c. They prowl.
6. How do horses move?
   a. They canter.
   b. They float.
   c. They ride.
7. How do monkeys move?
   a. They swing.
   b. They gallop.
   c. They run.
8. How do crabs move?
   a. They sidle.
   b. They wriggle.
   c. They slither.

B **Complete the sentences with these verbs.**

slithered   trotted   charged   prowled   leapt   hop

1. The horse slowly ____________ around the field.
2. The black mamba snake quietly ____________ towards its prey.
3. The herd of wildebeest ____________ at the leopard.
4. Do you know why kangaroos ____________?
5. We watched in awe as a pod of dolphins ____________ out of the ocean.
6. All night, the lion ____________ around the camp.

Grammar

Phrasal verbs

Read these sentences.

Bertie looked and learned as he ***grew up****.*

Vultures would ***finish off*** *anything that was left.*

He was thinking of ***giving up****.*

The words in bold are phrasal verbs.

A phrasal verb is a two-part verb that is made from a **verb** + a **preposition**, an **adverb** or **both**.

The meaning of a phrasal verb is different from the individual words that form it.

The secret to achieving one's goals is to never ***give up****. (give up = stop making an effort, different from the meanings of* ***give*** *and* ***up****)*

Here are some of the prepositions and adverbs that are often used in phrasal verbs:

in   up   on   away   round   over

out   down   off   back   through   by

A **Write the correct phrasal verb under each picture.**

do up	fall over	give back
hold back	knock over	put down
sit down	take off	wash up

____

____

____

____

____

____

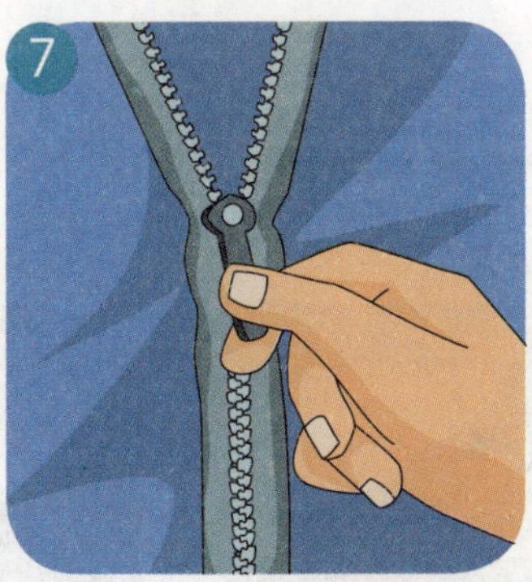

____

____

____

If the phrasal verb has an object, you can put the object after both words, or you can put it between them.

*Vultures **finished** the remains **off**.* *Vultures **finished off** the remains.*

If the object is a pronoun (such as *it, he, she,* etc), you always put the object between the words.

*Something **held** him **back**.*

B Rewrite the sentences using pronouns instead of the underlined words.

1. Put away your pencils.
2. Something held Bertie back.
3. Ameena put away her toys.
4. Anil took back his library book.
5. Mrs Khan is going to wake the children up.
6. Hanuman picked up the mountain.
7. I would advise against going on this trip.
8. While going to the library, I came across my old history teacher.
9. Put some warm clothes on before going outside.

Listening

An interview on the future of our planet

A Listen to Prita Shapur, a naturalist, talking about the future of the planet. Then, mark the statements as true (T) or false (F).

1. The biggest problem is the growing number of people on the planet. ______
2. We need fewer resources now than we did in the past. ______
3. We know how to build houses with less wood. ______

4. We know how to use less water to grow food. ______
5. Both governments and individuals are making changes that will help the environment. ______
6. Most people are trying to do something to protect the environment. ______
7. There is no reason for us to be hopeful about the future of our planet. ______
8. The new methods of farming require more chemicals than before. ______

B **Listen again and complete the sentences with words from Prita's answer to the interviewer's question.**

1. I'm basically quite optimistic about the future of the ______
2. The main challenge is that the world ______ is growing
3. We need to count on an increasing supply of food, water, wood, metal and all the other ______ that people need to live on
4. Amazing ______ in technology mean that we are now able to build cars that don't need petrol
5. We are now able to build houses that use very little ______
6. At the highest level, governments around the world are coming up with laws to protect ______
7. We have changed something about our behaviour for the good of the environment – whether ______

Speaking

Expressing an opinion

A **Which of these statements do you agree with? Write notes, and then speak to your partner about your views on each of the statements.**

1. Cars should be banned from city centres.
2. Petrol and diesel should be more expensive.
3. People are more important than animals.
4. It would not make any difference to the world if polar bears became extinct.

Use these phrases to help you express your opinions:

In my opinion/view ...
I think we should ...
I think it's terrible that ...
I think it's completely wrong that ...

Absolutely!
I think you're right.
You're absolutely right.
I completely agree with you.

I see what you mean, but ...
I'm afraid I don't agree with you at all.
I'm afraid I completely disagree with you.

B Work in pairs and prepare a speech on the topic, 'protection of wildlife'. Ensure that your speech includes these points:

- the meaning of wildlife
- what/who is causing harm to them
- details of species which are endangered and need protection
- data on species which have become extinct and the effect their extinction had on the ecosystem
- safety measures
- how you can help protect wildlife as a student

Writing

Writing a letter

Imagine that you are on holiday in the mountains or at the beach, surrounded by nature. Write a letter to your grandmother, describing the scenery around you.

Useful phrases

Greetings from ...!
We're having a great time in ...
We're staying/camping in ...
We're staying with ...
The weather's been fantastic ...
The scenery is breathtaking.
Tomorrow, we plan to ...
I don't want to come home!
I wish you were here.
Looking forward to seeing you.

Nature vocabulary

calm sea
clear skies
clear water
fresh mountain air
huge waves
miles of golden beaches
rolling hills (a lot of small, attractive hills)
sandy beach
snow-capped mountains

Follow this structure while writing the letter.

1. Greet your grandmother. Say where you are/who you are with.
2. Describe the place where you are staying, especially the scenery around you.
3. Talk about something you're planning to do.
4. End your letter with the appropriate salutation.

Poem

Pachamama is a goddess worshipped by some people in South America. She is also known as Mother Earth, and is sometimes regarded as nature itself. She is considered as kind and generous. The problem arises when people take too much from her.

What do you think happens when we exploit Mother Earth?

The Future

What does the future hold for us?
Smog[1]-filled skies and poison cars,
And broken land with useless dust
And nature's beauty behind bars.

Can I ever show my children,
(If they ever come my way)
The beauty of a sunset
At the ending of the day?

Can I walk into a forest,
And surround myself with trees,
Yet know that it will remain,
For me to visit as I please?

I know that I can today
Do all the things I've said,
But when today is yesterday,
Will all these things be dead?

This problem is enormous
As we gradually take heed[2],
So we must fix it quickly,
Using words and thoughts and deeds.

From the Pachamama

Wordfile

1. **Smog** is fog mixed with smoke.
2. When you **take heed**, you pay attention.

Poetry appreciation

Answer the questions.

1. The poet lists a few things that we can expect will happen if we continue to pollute our planet. Add three things of your own to the list.

   a. smog-filled skies
   b. poison cars
   c. ____________
   d. ____________
   e. ____________

2. 'And broken land with useless dust

   And nature's beauty behind bars.'

   Explain these lines in your own words.

3. 'But when today is yesterday,

   Will all these things be dead?'

   a. Explain what the poet means by 'when today is yesterday'.

   b. Why will all these things be dead?

   c. Can you think of two things that are dead already?

4. 'This problem is enormous.'

   What is the problem that is being referred to here? Do you agree that it's 'enormous'? What can be done to resolve the problem? Make notes and share them with your class.

5. Give an alternative title to this poem.

6. We should not selfishly take from Nature's resources. We should also give something back. Do you agree with the statement? Why/Why not? VBQ

Activity

Work in groups. Make a list of the ways in which you can reduce air pollution in your neighbourhood or city. Find out the following information:

- main sources of air pollution in your city
- what is being done by the government to deal with the problem
- what people can do to help
- number of private vehicles plying in your city daily
- eco-friendly forms of transport available in your city and how it helps combat pollution

Prepare a presentation on the topic. Support your presentation with visuals, posters and writing.

PROJECT 1

Wildlife Conservation

Many species of animals face extinction today due to human activities. Some species like the West African black rhino and the baiji dolphin have already become extinct, while the brown spider monkey and the Siamese crocodile have been declared as endangered species.

A **Look at these pictures and identify the endangered species. Find out how many members of each species are currently in existence. Has their number been increasing or decreasing in the last five years?**

1. 

____

2. 

____

3. 

____

4. 

____

5. 

____

6. 

____

B **The animals you identified in Exercise A and their habitats are at risk due to various reasons. Find out the reasons and note them down. Then, mention the attempts being made to conserve each species.**

1. Risk

____

Conservation efforts

____

____

2. Risk

____

____

Conservation efforts

____

____

3. Risk

Conservation efforts

4. Risk

Conservation efforts

5. Risk

Conservation efforts

6. Risk

Conservation efforts

C **Research and find out about some organizations which work for the conservation of wildlife. Then, arrange the information in the following table.**

Name of organization	Where and when it was set up	Kind of work it does	Head of the organization

D **In groups of four, select any one organization from exercise C and prepare a presentation on the work that they do.**

Dealing with a suspicious object

A Anil is at a metro station waiting for a train. He sees a bag lying unattended not very far from where he is standing. He looks around to see if there is someone to whom it might belong. But even after 15 minutes, no one comes to claim it. It is almost time for his train.

He knows that if he raises the alarm, the following could happen:

- His suspicion might be wrong; it might just be someone's handbag.
- The people on the platform might panic.
- The train officials might blame him for creating unnecessary panic and report the matter to the police.
- If proven wrong, he would be too embarrassed to board his train.

However, he is suspicious about the bag and fears that it might contain explosives.

What should he do? Should he:

1. inform the station authorities immediately? ☐
2. move as far as possible from the bag so that no harm can come to him? ☐
3. quickly board his train and forget about the bag? ☐
4. try to open the bag and see its contents? ☐
5. shout at everyone to move away from the bag? ☐
6. leave the station in case there is an explosion? ☐

B **The following is a list of things that you *should* and *should not* do to keep yourself and others safe. Put a tick [✓] next to the things that people *should* do. Put a cross [X] next to the things people *should not* do.**

1. Police: 100
2. Fire service: 101
3. Ambulance: 102

1. Keep a record of important phone numbers such as those for the police, the ambulance and the fire service. [ ]
2. Pick up unidentified objects that have been left unattended. [ ]
3. Leave your bags and other goods unattended in public places. [ ]
4. Be cautious of strangers. [ ]
5. Check for unidentified objects under your seat in cinemas and while using public transport. [ ]
6. Inform the authorities, even if you have only the smallest suspicion. [ ]
7. Start shouting and creating panic. [ ]
8. Check the contents of an unattended bag or closed containers. [ ]
9. Be extra cautious at crowded and busy market places. [ ]
10. Do not think about others; just try and save yourself. [ ]

C **Discuss how you would behave if you were in Anil's situation, and found a suspicious object.**

• 4 Food

In this unit, I will ...

- practise pronunciation of unstressed *to*
- learn some words for fruits and vegetables
- learn about the usage of *must, mustn't, have to* and *don't have to*
- listen to a conversation about food allergies
- prepare and give a short talk on healthy eating

Warm-up

A **Answer the clues 1–7 and complete in the crossword to make a word in the blue box which relates to the theme of this unit.**

Clues

1. This grain is used to make bread.
2. This describes food that is not stale or old
3. This is food eaten between meals.
4. This white powder is used to make chapatis, bread and cakes.
5. This is a place where you can buy all sorts of different goods.
6. This is the room where you cook.
7. This place sells bread and cakes.

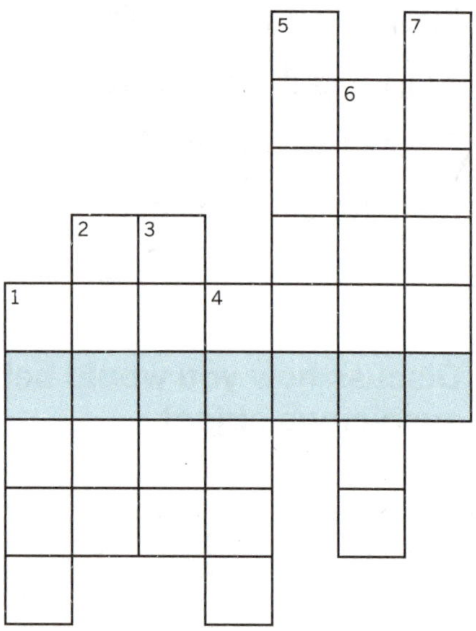

B **Make a list of words related to baking, such as the things that you can bake, or the ingredients that you usually use when you are baking.**

1. ____________
2. ____________
3. ____________
4. ____________
5. ____________
6. ____________
7. ____________
8. ____________
9. ____________
10. ____________

Reading 1

Can you imagine a teenager successfully running his or her own business?

Read about Zach, a teenager who has his own business, baking healthy bread and cakes. Zach's story appears on a US children's health website.

Zach's Story

I love great food – fresh, local food that doesn't travel for days before it gets to you! I've turned this interest into a healthy baking business that's expanded and grown in popularity. I use local farm fresh eggs, organic spelt flour[1] and real butter. No preservatives. No trans fats[2]. If I can't pronounce it, I don't eat it!

I discovered a love for baking and cooking when I was eight (I'm now fifteen). Around that time, my mum found out she has a wheat allergy, which means she can't eat the type of flour most people eat. But she is only allergic to wheat, not gluten[3], so she can have a certain type of flour called spelt flour.

Because she was missing many of her favourite foods, I started experimenting with spelt flour to see if I could make some of the things she was missing. Spelt flour has a different type of protein that is easier to digest, so it's a great alternative for some people who are allergic to wheat.

I found out that I loved working in the kitchen. Soon I was making many of the meals and all the baked goods for our house.

Opportunity knocks – then knocks again

I started working with Martin Ruiz, who had a bakery. He sold mostly at a local farmers' market[4]. At first I worked at the market, but I soon started baking.

Martin decided to pursue other business interests and asked if I wanted to run the bakery for him. I was thrilled! A few months went by, then one day at the market I saw a notice that a national healthy grocery

Wordfile

1. **Spelt flour** is a type of wheat.
2. **Trans fats** are a type of fat that you find in some prepared foods, such as cake. A lot of people think they are not healthy.
3. **Gluten** is a protein that is present in wheat.
4. A **farmer's market** is a market at which farmers sell the fruit, vegetables, eggs, etc that they have produced.

chain was looking for local vendors[5]. Up until this point I had been baking wheat products only for farmers' markets. But this opportunity fitted with my plans to provide fresh-baked, snack-sized spelt products for people who can't eat wheat.

I submitted an application and samples to see if my spelt products would meet their needs[6]. I waited for about a month and then the notice came that I had been accepted! Over the next few months, things started moving fast. I met with the grocery chain's regional people. I had to make decisions on labels, packaging, and which products to ship first. I had to find wholesale[7] vendors willing to sell me bulk[8] ingredients, like spelt flour.

Fitting a business in with school

I am home-schooled[9]. Running the business is part of my education. I have to do book-keeping[10] to track invoices[11] and expenses. I have to calculate margins (how much money I need to make per item). I have to plan ahead for expenses like flour deliveries, propane[12], packaging, and labels. I have to stay on top[13] of these things or I may run out of something important and not be able to make a delivery.

When you are in business, the most important thing is keeping your word[14]. I always focus on making the best product and getting it to the stores. Things go wrong, but you have to keep going. I've been through storms that I thought would blow my kitchen right over, lost electricity or water (both things shut you down for a while). Sometimes things go wrong that later turn out to be the best thing. I call these things happy accidents.

I spend about 17 hours a week (including book-keeping) on my business. I plan things carefully so I can get a lot done as quickly as possible. And I'm learning management skills: my dad delivers my products since I don't have my licence yet. My mum helps with lots of details, including driving me to my kitchen 20 miles away.

Wordfile

5. A **vendor** is someone who sells something.
6. If something **meets someone's needs**, it is exactly what they need.
7. **Wholesale** means selling in large quantities to shops and businesses and not directly to customers.
8. **Bulk** amounts are large amounts, usually bought by a business.
9. **Home-schooled** children are taught at home by their parents instead of at school.
10. **Book-keeping** is the activity of keeping records of the money that a company spends and receives.
11. **Invoices** are bills.
12. **Propane** is a gas that people use as a fuel.
13. To **stay on top** of a situation is to continue to manage it successfully.
14. If you **keep your word**, you do what you have promised to do.

My two brothers, Robert and Duncan, help me with packaging and dishes. My older brother Robert drives me when my mum can't, and is great at fixing things that break in the kitchen. Every kitchen needs a good maintenance[15] person.

I'm busy, but I still have time for other interests. In my spare time, I am restoring a 1968 Volkswagen Karman Ghia. My whole family loves working on cars.

My philosophy on healthy eating is: 'Go local! Eat fresh (no preservatives or artificial anything). Try new things. And support local business and companies. Transporting food hundreds of miles wastes resources.'

Wordfile

15. **Maintenance** is the process of keeping something in good condition.

Comprehension 1

A Arrange the sentences in the order of events in the story.

1. Zach started baking using a different type of flour. ______
2. Zach started to run the bakery. ______
3. Zach's mum found out that wheat made her ill and she could no longer eat it. ______
4. A national food company agreed to start selling Zach's products. ______
5. Zach started working for a man who owned a bakery. ______

B Circle the correct option.

1. Zach's mum can't eat

   a. gluten. b. the type of wheat that most people eat. c. spelt flour.

2. Zach started baking with spelt flour because

   a. he wanted to make bread and cakes that his mother could enjoy.

   b. spelt flour is cheaper than other types of flour.

   c. spelt flour tastes better than other types of flour.

3. Zach soon started making

   a. all the meals in his house.

   b. all the bread and cake in his house.

   c. all of his mother's meals.

4. Zach says the main thing in business is to
   a. do what you have promised you will do.
   b. be polite.
   c. keep believing that you will succeed.

C Answer the questions.

1. According to Zach, when things go wrong with your business, what do you have to do?
2. What are 'happy accidents'?
3. How do Zach's healthy snacks get to the shops where they are sold?
4. According to Zach, why is it wrong to take food to places that are hundreds of miles away?

Comprehension 2

Zach says: 'Sometimes things go wrong that later turn out to be the best thing. I call these things happy accidents.'

VBQ **Can you think of a proverb which can be applied to the situations described by Zach? Is it right to depend on 'happy accidents' to solve our problems, or should we try our best to avoid the chances of things going wrong?**

Vocabulary check

A Find a word in the text that ...

1. means something that you make or grow in order to sell. p____________
2. means the paper or plastic that something is in when you buy it. p____________
3. refers to a condition that makes you ill if you eat or touch a particular thing.
   a____________
4. describes food which is grown or made in a natural way, without chemicals.
   o____________
5. means something which is added to a food to make it last longer. p____________
6. means to test a new idea or method. e____________
7. means extremely pleased and excited. t____________
8. means to grow bigger. e____________

B **Complete the sentences using words from Exercise A. Use the correct form of the words.**

1. I don't like using the same recipe every time I cook. I prefer to ____________ with different ingredients and see which of them works best.
2. They sell a range of ____________ – fruit and vegetables but also bread, cakes, nuts and dried fruit.
3. There's so much plastic ____________ around food these days and it all just ends up in the bin.
4. Twenty per cent of the population have food ____________ of one sort or another and can't eat particular types of food.
5. The label on the jar said the food was organic and contained no ____________.

Language skills

Idioms

*When you are in business, the most important thing is **keeping your word**.*

Zach uses the idiom *to keep your word*, meaning 'to do what you have promised to do'.

A **There are a lot of idioms with *word*. In your dictionary, look under the entry 'word' and find the following idioms. Then, match the idioms with their meanings.**

Idioms	Meanings
1. in a word	a. using exactly the same words as the person who said them
2. take someone's word for it	b. by people telling each other
3. word for word	c. in as few words as possible
4. from the word go	d. believe that someone is telling the truth
5. by word of mouth	e. from the beginning of a period of time

B **Complete the sentences with the idioms from Exercise A.**

1. Riyad and Azad have both worked on the project ________________
2. 'So did Anjali enjoy her first day at school?' '________________, no.'
3. Information like this often spreads ________________
4. Vani will be of no help and you'll end up doing all the work yourself, ________________
5. I can tell you exactly what she said, ________________

Pronunciation: *have to* and *has to*

A **Listen to Zach talking about all the things that he has to do. Notice the way he pronounces 'have to'. He does not emphasize the 'oo' sound in 'to'. Instead, he says something that sounds like 'hafta'.**

B **Repeat these sentences, pronouncing 'have to' as 'hafta'.**

1. I have to go now.
2. You'll have to tell her.
3. We have to get up very early.
4. Vani and Babu have to be back by five o'clock.
5. Remember, we have to get Imran a present.

C **In a similar way, we pronounce 'has to' as 'hazta'. Write four sentences starting with 'Zach has to ...'. Then practise saying the sentences with a partner.**

1. ______________________________
2. ______________________________
3. ______________________________
4. ______________________________

Reading 2

The original story starts with these lines from Bill, the narrator and main character of the story:

Oranges! I loved them. I used to eat them all day and every day. But one day, a policeman found seventeen oranges in my pockets. He locked me up and I have never eaten an orange again.

What do you imagine happened to those seventeen oranges? Why do you think Bill suddenly stopped eating his favourite fruit?

Read the story and see if you guessed correctly.

Seventeen Oranges

Me and my friend Clem worked at the docks[1]. All day we loaded and unloaded things from the ships.

I was not really a thief. But I usually left the docks with something under my apron.

When there was a banana boat in the docks, I drove my little cart beside it. Sometimes bunches of bananas fell to the ground. I always picked up the bananas and quickly hid them under my apron[2].

Wordfile

1. A **dock** is an area of water next to land where ships go so that people can get on or off them.
2. An **apron** is a piece of clothing that you wear over the front of your normal clothes, to stop them from getting dirty.

I only took things when they fell down, but Clem was more daring. One day, he played a great trick on the policeman, PC Pongo.

Clem opened his box. The cat jumped out like a flash and ran back to the ship.

A few minutes later, Clem came back with the same box, looking angry and holding down the lid tightly. PC Pongo was laughing.

As soon as he was out of sight, Clem ran all the way home. He opened the box. Inside was a large Dutch cheese.

I like cheese. I like bananas. But most of all, I like oranges. One day, I was carrying away oranges in my apron when my apron string broke.

The policeman saw my pockets stuffed full of oranges. He took me into his hut and emptied out my pockets.

I was very frightened, but I kept quiet. I had read a lot of detective stories. I knew that the best plan was to say nothing.

PC Pongo locked the door and left.

I was very worried. I would lose my job! Perhaps I would go to prison. What would my father say? There was no escape. Then I heard a voice in my head.

I picked up an orange, peeled and ate it.

But there was no time to peel. I cut the oranges into large pieces and swallowed them one after the other.

I heard footsteps coming. I quickly ate up the last bits of orange and swallowed.

Wordfile

3. A **pip** is one of the small, hard seeds in a fruit such as an apple or an orange.
4. **Peel** is the skin of a fruit such as a lemon or an apple.

I was starting to feel very sick by now, but I stayed quiet.

He searched me, he searched the room. Finally he understood what had happened.

I said nothing.

Pongo became angry and shouted at me, but in the end, he had to let me go.

I told Clem all about the seventeen oranges.

But I wasn't thinking about PC Pongo, then.

Bill Naughton

About the author

Bill Naughton, (1910–1992), was born in Ireland. He wrote a lot of plays, novels, short stories and children's books. The characters in his writing usually worked hard and were quite poor.

Comprehension 1

A Match the sentence halves in columns A and B to describe what happened in the story.

A	B
1. The boy often hid bananas and other things	a. he could see oranges in his pockets.
2. Clem once stole	b. in a hut for half an hour.
3. The policeman caught the boy because	c. in his apron.
4. PC Pongo locked the boy	d. eating seventeen oranges.
5. The boy felt ill after	e. a chunk of cheese.

B **Read the quotes from the story and answer the questions.**

1. 'Mind your cat doesn't escape again!'
   a. Who said these words and to whom?
   b. Why did he say this?
   c. Did the cat actually escape again? Why?
2. You stole these oranges! What have you got to say for yourself?
   a. Who said this?
   b. What made him notice the stolen oranges?
   c. What happened next?
3. 'Where are the oranges?'
   a. Who said this and to whom?
   b. What had the listener done with the oranges?
   c. Why did he do so?
4. 'Pongo locked you in that hut for half an hour! He had no right to do that.'
   a. Who said these words and to whom?
   b. Who was Pongo and why did he lock up the listener of the lines above?
   c. Do you think he deserved to be locked up? Give a reason.

Comprehension 2

Answer the questions.

1. What sort of character is PC Pongo? Do you like him? Why/Why not?
2. What do we know about Clem's character?
3. If you were caught in a situation like the boy, what would you do? Why? VBQ
4. 'Here's the thief!' VBQ
   a. Is the boy a thief?
   b. Did he do something really bad?
   c. Do you feel sorry for him?
5. Do you think the boy stole the oranges because he was hungry, or out of greed? Is it right to steal food when someone is very hungry? Give reasons for your answer. VBQ

Vocabulary

A Complete the sentences using these words.

searched	said	believe	told	swallowed	found

1. The boy only stole the things that he ____________ on the docks.
2. When PC Pongo asked the boy about the oranges, the boy ____________ nothing.
3. The boy peeled the seventeen oranges and then ____________ them.
4. When he came back, Pongo ____________ the hut for the seventeen oranges, but found nothing.
5. Pongo could not ____________ that anyone could eat seventeen oranges.
6. The boy ____________ his friend, Clem, about eating the oranges.

B Read these two extracts from newspaper reports. They both contain words related to crime. Read the sentences to understand what the words mean.

The police thought that it was Koy who **stole** the money, but they could not **prove** it as there was no **evidence**. He was sent to **prison** for nine months for stealing cars.

There was a **theft** at the bank on Tuesday. **Witnesses** say they saw a man running out of the building, carrying two big bags. **Detectives** are still searching for the **thief**.

Match the crime words from the extracts with their meanings.

1. ____________: a building where criminals have to stay
2. ____________: to show that something is definitely true
3. ____________: a thing that shows that something is true

4. ______________: a person who sees something happen, especially a crime or an accident
5. ______________: to take something from someone without their permission
6. ______________: someone whose job is to find out who has done a crime
7. ______________: the act of taking something from someone without their permission
8. ______________: someone who takes and keeps things from other people without their permission

C **Solve the crossword.**

Clues

Across

1. metal rings put on a person's wrist by the police
2. to give money to someone in order to get something done dishonestly
3. when the police tries to find facts about a crime

Down

4. document issued by the court giving the police the power to do something
5. a criminal act

Grammar

Using *have to* and *must*

We use **have to** and **must** to say that we are required to do something because of a rule or that we need to do something because it is important.

*We **have to** wear a uniform to school. (rule)*

*The treasurer **has to** keep a record of all the money that has been spent. (rule)*

*I **must** call Sally this evening. (important)*

*You **must** give Annie her book back. (important)*

We use **have to** when we are talking about general rules that other people have made.

We use **must** to show that the rule is very important, or when we are talking to ourselves in a determined way.

*We **have to** be at school by eight o'clock*. (A teacher has made this rule for everyone.)

*I **must** swallow all the oranges, I thought*. (The speaker is talking to himself in a determined way.)

We can use **have to** in the past, but we cannot use **must** in the past.

*When I was a child, we **had to** stand up when the teacher entered the class.*

A Read each sentence. Write *C* if it is correct or *W* if it is wrong.

1. I must remember to send Uncle Robert a birthday card! ______
2. I must take these books back to the library. ______
3. Last week I had to do eight pieces of homework! ______
4. Last year our class must have read a whole novel in English. ______
5. Parents have to pay for their children's education. ______
6. Everyone had to stand in front of the class and give a short talk. ______

B Match the first part of the sentences in column A with the second part in column B.

A	B
1. It was raining hard so we	a. must listen to her.
2. Your teacher will give you instructions so you	b. must take some blankets.
3. If you bring money with you, you	c. must keep it somewhere safe.
4. It will get cold at night so you	d. had to go inside.

We use **don't have to** when we are saying that it is not necessary to do something.

*I like Sundays because I **don't have to** go to school.*

*Zach **doesn't have to** mend his own equipment; his brother does it.*

We use **mustn't** to say that something is not allowed and it is very important not to do that thing.

*This is a secret. If I tell you, you **mustn't** tell anyone!*

*You really **mustn't** swim in the river. It's too dangerous.*

C Underline the correct option in each sentence.

1. We have to leave at nine o'clock so you **mustn't/don't have to** be late.
2. Come if you want to, but you **mustn't/don't have to**.
3. You **mustn't/don't have to** talk when the teacher is speaking.
4. You **mustn't/don't have to** leave the class without your teacher's permission.
5. Please help yourselves to food. You **mustn't/don't have to** ask.
6. During the visit to the museum, you can wear your school uniform if you want to but you **mustn't/don't have to**.
7. Your father will be worried about you so, you **mustn't/don't have to** forget to call him when you arrive there.
8. He's very rich. So he **mustn't/doesn't have to** work.

D Complete these sentences using phrases containing *mustn't* or *don't have to*.

1. You can look at the pictures in the gallery but you ____________________
2. Remember you have to get up really early tomorrow morning to catch the train, so you ____________________
3. We'll have plenty of food, so you ____________________
4. Your grandmother is expecting you at three o'clock, so you ____________________
5. Well, I'm going to do some baking, but ____________________
6. It's Raju's birthday next Wednesday, so I ____________________
7. A lot of people in our country don't have enough to eat. So we ____________________
8. Rahul uses the books his sister had handed down to him, so he ____________________
9. We will book the tickets for the film beforehand, so ____________________

Listening

Allergies

A **Listen to Sally talking to her new friend, Farida. Sally is telling Farida about her food allergy and the problems that it causes for her.**

Circle the correct option.

1. Sally has been allergic to chickpeas
   a. all her life.
   b. for six or seven years.
   c. for six or seven months.
2. If Sally eats chickpeas
   a. her mouth and lips become itchy.
   b. she gets a headache.
   c. she feels sick.
3. Sally can eat in restaurants but she has to
   a. take her own food.
   b. avoid all vegetables dishes.
   c. avoid dishes with chickpeas in them.
4. In a restaurant, Sally's mother
   a. talks to the waiter to make sure that the dishes do not contain chickpeas.
   b. tastes the dishes first to make sure there are no chickpeas in them.
   c. looks in each dish to make sure it is safe for Sally to eat.
5. Sally says it is more difficult if you are
   a. allergic to brinjal.
   b. allergic to an ingredient that is found in lots of foods.
   c. allergic to vegetables generally.

B **Listen again and complete the sentences. Use these words from the text.**

avoid	allergy	itchy	allergic	mild

1. Sally is ____________ to chickpeas.
2. Luckily, her allergy is only ____________ and does not make her seriously ill.

3. Sally tries hard to ____________ chickpeas.
4. Chickpeas make Sally's mouth and lips feel ____________.
5. Sally read about a girl who has a milk ____________.

Speaking

Healthy eating

Work with a partner. Prepare a short talk of about two minutes on the subject of healthy eating. Use the ideas below to help you.

- the types of food we should eat more
- the types of food we should eat less
- the types of food we should avoid completely
- how much food we should eat
- when we should eat
- the types of meal we eat, for example, snacks or proper family meals at the table
- how we cook our food
- where we shop for food

Useful phrases

Try to eat more ...

Try to eat less ...

Make sure you eat ...

Eat *at least ...

**Cut down on ...

Eat fruit instead of ...

Try boiling ... instead of frying ...

*__At least__ means 'not less than' a particular amount.

**To __cut down on__ a particular food is to eat less of it.

Writing

Writing an email

You made lunch for a friend recently. The friend enjoyed it very much and has emailed you to ask for the recipe for the dish that you prepared.

Write an informal email giving instructions on how to prepare the dish.

Remember to greet your friend first and thank him or her for saying nice things about the dish.

You can start like this:

To
From
Subject

Hi Jia,

So nice to hear from you. Thank you for your message.

I'm glad you enjoyed the dish so much. Of course I will share the recipe with you. It's my mother's recipe. This is how it is made ...

Useful phrases

Add a little ... to the ...	Fry the ... in a little oil/butter.
Put the ... into a bowl and ...	Fry/Boil ... until they are ...
Mix the ... with the ...	Slice the ... into thin pieces.
Bake for half an hour.	When that is done, ...

Useful verbs

bake	fry	peel
beat	grill	slice
boil	heat	stir
chop	melt	

Remember to use these words too

First ...

Next ...

Finally ...

Poem

Do you ever think about things that are in the past? Do you like to remember good times or bad times?

Read this thought-provoking poem about the dreams of the bones of a fish.

Fishbones Dreaming

Fishbones lay in a smelly bin.
He was a head, a backbone and a tail.
Soon the cats would be in for him.

He didn't like to be this way.
He shut his eyes and dreamed back.

Back to when he was fat, and hot on a plate.
Beside green beans, with lemon juice squeezed on him.
And a man with a knife
And fork raised, about to eat him.

He didn't like to be this way.
He shut his eyes and dreamed back.

Back to when he was frozen in the freezer.
With cutlets and minced meat[1] and prawns.
Three months he was in there.

He didn't like to be this way.
He shut his eyes and dreamed back.

Back to when he was squirming[2] in a net,
With thousands of other fish, on the deck of a boat.
And the rain falling
Wasn't wet enough to breathe in.

He didn't like to be this way.
He shut his eyes and dreamed back.

Back to when he was darting[3] through the sea,
Past crabs and jellyfish, and others like himself.
Or surfacing to jump for flies
And feel the sun on his face.

He liked to be this way.
He dreamed hard to try and stay there.

Matthew Sweeney

Wordfile

1. **Minced meat** is meat that has been cut and chopped into very small pieces.
2. When a person or animal **squirms**, they twist their body from side to side because they are in pain or trying to escape.
3. When a person or animal **darts** somewhere, they move there suddenly and quickly.

About the poet

Matthew Sweeney (b. 1951) is an Irish poet. He has published many poetry collections for adults and children, and two children's novels. He has held several fellowships and has won many awards for literature. He was nominated for the T. S. Eliot Award for his book, *Black Moon* (2007).

Poetry appreciation

A Answer the questions.

1. Who lay in a 'smelly bin'?
2. For how long was he in a freezer?
3. Name two things he didn't want to dream about.
4. 'He didn't like to be this way.

   He shut his eyes and dreamed back'.

   a. Who didn't like to be this way?

   b. Which way didn't he like to be? Mention any one of the ways.

   c. Why do you think he didn't like to be 'this way'?

   d. Why do you think he closed his eyes and dreamed back?
5. 'He liked to be this way.

   He dreamed hard to try and stay there'.

   a. Which way did he like to be?

   b. Why did he dream 'hard' to stay there?
6. Name two of the creatures that Fishbones swam with.
7. Notice that the poet uses these lines repeatedly.

   'He didn't like to be this way.

   He shut his eyes and dreamed back'.

   The repetition of phrases in a song or poem, especially at the end of each stanza, is called **refrain**.

   Why do you think the poet repeats these lines? What effect does this produce?
8. There are several instances of flashback in the poem. According to you, what purpose does it serve?
9. VBQ Do you feel sorry for Fishbones? Why?

B **Read another example of a refrain.**

1. These verses have been taken from 'The Brook' by Lord Alfred Tennyson. Notice the refrain used in the poem.

Till last by Philip's farm I flow
To join the brimming river,
For men may come and men may go,
But I go on for ever.
(third verse)

And out again I curve and flow
To join the brimming river,
For men may come and men may go,
But I go on for ever.
(last verse)

Have you read the poem? Try to find it and read it to the rest of the class.

Activity

A balanced diet consists of a particular percentage of each food group.

A **Write the names of two food items for each of the following groups.**

Proteins	Fats	Carbohydrates	Vitamins	Minerals

B **Make a note of what you eat for breakfast, lunch and dinner. Calculate the amount of calorie intake using the following calorie chart and decide whether you have a balanced diet. Then, work with a partner. Read each other's findings and identify similarities and differences in your diets.**

Item	Quantity	Calories
Boiled egg	1	80
Slice of bread with butter	1	90
Chapati	1	60
Rice	1 cup	150
Dal	1 cup	150
Vegetable	1 cup	150
Chicken	1 cup	175
Milk with sugar	1 cup	75

5 Sports

In this unit, I will ...

- learn when to use *play*, *do* and *go* when talking about different sports
- learn some terms related to sports
- learn about the use of the active and the passive voice and practise articles
- listen to, and role-play an interview with a sportsperson
- learn to write a report

Warm-up

A **Complete the crossword using the clues. The words are all connected with athletics (= sports such as running and jumping).**

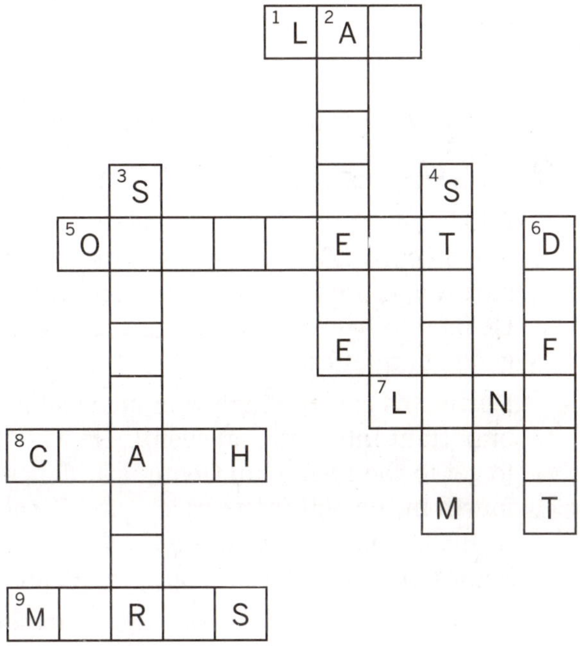

Clues

Across

1. one turn around a racecourse
5. the person who is against you in a sports competition
7. the finishing _________________; the mark on the ground that shows the end of the race
8. someone whose job is to train sportspersons
9. 'On your _________________, get set, go!' said the starter to the runners at the beginning of the race.

Down

2. someone who is good at sports, especially sports such as running, jumping and throwing things
3. someone who watches a sports event
4. a large area for playing sports with seats all around it
6. a verb meaning 'to beat someone'

B **Work with a partner. Make a list of team sports. Then, make a list of individual sports. Which type of sport do you prefer?**

C **Is it more difficult to succeed in team sports than in individual sports? Discuss with your partner.**

Reading 1

You are going to read an extract from the autobiography of famous athlete, Milkha Singh. He is also called the 'Flying Sikh'. Do you know when and why he was given this title?

About the author

Milkha Singh was born in 1935 in Govindpura, Punjab Province. Singh's early life was not easy. His parents died during the partition of India, and Singh then moved from Pakistan to India. He later joined the Indian army where he discovered that he was good at athletics.

During his career, Singh won medals for his running at many important international events. He was the first Indian man to get to the final of an Olympic athletics event when he came fourth in the 400-metre race at the Rome 1960 Olympic Games. In 1959, Singh was awarded the Padma Shri (one of India's highest honours) for his sporting achievements.

The Flying Sikh

Soon after the National Games, our team had received an invitation from the Pakistani government for the Indo-Pak Sports Meet. I was returning to the land where I was born, where I had lost my home and most of my family in the riots[1] after the India-Pakistan partition. The fear that the visit would revive[2] those horrible memories troubled me. I did not

Wordfile

1. A **riot** is an occasion when a group of people behave violently in a public place.
2. If an experience **revives** a memory, it makes you start to remember something that happened in the past.

want to go, but Pandit Nehru persuaded me, saying that this visit was for the honour of our country and that I was going there as an ambassador[3] of India. The others in our team felt as I did, as we reluctantly[4] travelled to the border at Attari via Amritsar. When we reached Pakistan, the welcoming committee at the border greeted us warmly and then we were taken by bus to the Faletti's Hotel in Lahore.

Days before the Meet opened, headlines in newspapers carried large-print notices that said:

INDO-PAK ATHLETE DUEL
ABDUL KHALIQ TO MEET MILKHA SINGH

The Meet was declared open by the President of Pakistan, General Ayub Khan, at the Gaddafi stadium. There were more than 30,000 spectators in the men's section and several thousand more *burqa*-clad[5] ladies in the women's. At this event I was once again pitted against[6] my old opponent, Abdul Khaliq, whom I had defeated in the Tokyo Games.

The crowd's excitement levels were high as they eagerly waited for the moment when their hero would defeat me. In this Meet too, like in the Tokyo Games, Khaliq won the 100 meters, and I, the 400-metre race. The deciding[7] race was the 200-metre one. My team-mates reassured me by saying there was no way that I could lose, my technique was too finely honed[8] and my timing was much better than the one at Tokyo. But as usual, on the day of the race, I woke up feeling feverish. I was shivering, either because I was unwell, or by memories of those terrible days that still troubled me. Instead of feeling sorry for myself, I forced myself to get up and go to the stadium.

Once at the stadium, the Pakistanis greeted Khaliq by shouting, 'Long Live Abdul Khaliq'. The entire audience kept cheering for him as he walked in before me. There was pin-drop silence as we stood at the starting line waiting for the race to begin. The silence was oppressive[9]. The starter shouted, 'On your marks ...,' fired the gun and the race began. The audience suddenly awoke and began to chant: 'Abdul Kahliq *zindabad*'. Khaliq was ahead of me but I caught up before we had completed

Milkha Singh in 2014

Wordfile

3. If you are an **ambassador** for your organization or nation, you represent it at an event.
4. When you do something **reluctantly**, you do it against your wish.
5. If someone is **clad** in a particular item of clothing, they are wearing it.
6. If you are **pitted against** someone, you are competing against him or her.
7. A **deciding** race is one that will prove who is the winner of the series.
8. A skill that is **honed** has been practised many times and is now perfect.
9. Something that is **oppressive** makes you feel anxious or depressed.

the first 100 metres. We were shoulder-to-shoulder, then surprisingly, Khaliq seemed to slacken[10] and I surged[11] ahead as if on wings. I finished the 200 metres about ten yards ahead of Khaliq, clocking the 20.7 seconds that equalled the world record. My coach, Ranbir Singh, the manager and all my team members leapt to their feet in jubilation[12]. I was embraced, thumped on the back and lifted on to their shoulders as they expressed their happiness both vocally and physically.

It was indeed a joyful day for us. Khaliq was so devastated that he lay on the ground weeping pitifully. I patted his back and tried to console him by saying that victory and defeat were part of the same game and should not be taken to heart[13], but he felt humiliated by the fact that he had been defeated in his own country.

After the race, I ran a victory lap of the stadium, while loudspeakers announced: 'The athlete running before you is Milkha Singh. He does not run, he flies. His victory will be recorded in Pakistan's sports' history, and we confer[14] the title of "Flying Sikh" on him.' It was General Ayub Khan who coined the title 'Flying Sikh', when he congratulated me saying, '*Tum daudey nahi, udhey ho* – you did not run, but flew!'

Milkha Singh with Sonia Sanwalka

Wordfile

10. To **slacken** is to become slower and less powerful.
11. To **surge** means to move forwards suddenly and quickly.
12. **Jubilation** is great happiness and celebration about something good that has happened.
13. If you **take to heart** what someone says or does to you, you are affected and upset by it.
14. If you **confer** a title or honour **on** someone, you give it to them. *(formal)*

Comprehension 1

A Circle the correct answer.

1. The Pakistani government invited Singh to take part in the Indo-Pak Sports Meet. At first, Singh was
   a. unwilling to go.
   b. excited about going.
   c. excited but nervous too.
2. Singh decided to go to the Indo-Pak Sports Meet because
   a. the other athletes in his team encouraged him to go.
   b. then Prime Minister of India at the time, Pandit Nehru, encouraged him to go.
   c. his coach encouraged him to go.

3. Singh had beaten Abdul Khaliq once before in a race in
   a. Tokyo.
   b. London.
   c. Rome.
4. The audience at the stadium shouted encouragement to
   a. Abdul Khaliq and Milkha Singh.
   b. Milkha Singh only.
   c. Abdul Khaliq only.
5. The 200-metre race was
   a. the first of three that the two men ran.
   b. the last of three that the two men ran.
   c. the second of three that the two men ran.
6. At the start of the race
   a. Abdul Khaliq was in front.
   b. Milkha Singh was in front.
   c. both men were running shoulder-to-shoulder.

B Are the statements true (T) or false (F)?

1. The front pages of the newspapers announced that the two men, Milkha Singh and Abdul Khaliq, were going to compete. ________
2. Everyone in the crowd expected Khaliq to beat Singh. ________
3. Abdul Khaliq had won the 400-metre race in the Tokyo Games. ________
4. Singh tried to comfort Khaliq after the race. ________
5. Khaliq felt better after Singh had said a few things to console him. ________
6. Singh ran twice round the track after winning the race. ________

C Answer the questions.

1. How much time did Milkha Singh take to complete the race? What is the significance of that time?
2. After the race, there was an announcement on the loudspeakers. What was the announcement? What did it show about the way that the Pakistani people responded to Milkha Singh's achievement?
3. Who gave Milkha Singh the title 'Flying Sikh'? Why?

Comprehension 2

VBQ **A** If a person who loses a race or game is 'gracious in defeat', they are pleasant and show respect to the person who has defeated them.

1. Were the Pakistani President and people gracious in defeat?
2. Have you ever seen a sportsperson or a team who was *not* gracious in defeat?
3. Is winning more important than participation? Give reasons for your answer.

VBQ **B** A true sportsperson treats his/her opponent respectfully even after defeating them. Do you think Milkha Singh behaved like a true sportsperson? Why/Why not?

Vocabulary check

When two or more words are often used together, we call this group of words a **collocation**.

A **Form collocations by matching the verbs in column A with the nouns that come after them in column B.**

A	B
1. to congratulate	a. a dog
2. to fire	b. a gun
3. to pat	c. a guest
4. to express	d. a new phrase
5. to greet	e. the winner
6. to coin	f. your feelings

B **Choose any four collocations from Exercise A and use them in sentences of your own.**

C **Choose the correct nouns that go with the given adjectives to form collocations.**

1. delicious ________

   a. room b. tea c. food

2. warm ___________

   a. clothes b. software c. choice

3. loud ___________

   a. sleep b. music c. smell

4. strong ________

    a. coffee   b. water   c. cake

5. heavy ________

    a. night   b. bag   c. exam

6. regular ________

    a. exercise   b. table   c. soap

Language skills

Using *play*, *do* and *go*

We use the verbs **play**, **do** and **go** with sports and leisure activities.

1. We use **play** with team sports, such as football, and with sports such as badminton, in which there is a ball or an object like a ball. We also use **play** for activities such as chess in which two people or teams play against each other.

    *Do you **play** cricket?*   *Riyaz is learning to **play** chess.*

2. We use **do** with individual sports in which there is no ball, such as athletics and boxing. We also use **do** with leisure activities, such as puzzles.

    *Amit **does** a lot of weightlifting in his spare time.*

    *Children generally like to **do** puzzles.*

3. We use **go** with sports and leisure activities ending in **-ing**. These are sports like swimming or running.

    *We're **going** swimm**ing** this afternoon.*

Notice that we do not use the verb **make** with sports or leisure activities.

A Put these popular sports and leisure activities in the correct columns in this table.

cricket   football   hockey   tennis   chess   boxing   table tennis   weightlifting
basketball   volleyball   kabaddi   badminton   archery   golf   wrestling   swimming

play	do	go

Reading 2

You are going to read a short story about a boy who is taking part in an inter-school sports competition.

The Take-off Board

He wouldn't make it – not today – here in this park that had the best athletic track he had ever seen. He knew he could beat them, all of them – but he wouldn't. They wouldn't let him! They were against him. He could feel it in the air, could see it in their eyes, in the way they turned and moved away from him, demonstrating a boisterous[1] comradeship[2] that left him out.

He fell into a warm-up run, conscious[3] of his legs growing heavy as lead, not moving the way they usually did, with easy, long strides. He stopped by the long-jump pit, avoiding looking at the boys around. Rattan Mehta, the superstar, tall, handsome, with muscles hard as steel, was laughing. They were all laughing at him.

He wished he hadn't come to Delhi. He wished he were back in Cochin, back with his friends, running a friendly race, already leading with great ease.

'Come on, boys, get going. Over there to the long-jump pit.' The coach collected the boys with a sweeping gesture of his arm. 'Don't waste time, fellows. We have to get ready for the interschool sports day.'

Pushing each other jovially[4], the boys lined up in front of the pit. He trailed behind, listening to the enthusiastic shouts and the encouraging remarks of the coach: 'Fine jump, Madan; keep it up, son!'

He bit his lip nervously. Soon it would be his turn, his chance to show them.

'Next!'

His turn, his long-awaited turn. He sprinted into a run, his eyes fixed on the

Wordfile

1. **Boisterous** behaviour is lively and noisy.
2. **Comradeship** is the friendship that exists between people who work together as part of a team.
3. If you are **conscious of** something, you know about it.
4. If you do something **jovially**, you do it in a happy and friendly way.

take-off board. A few more strides, one – two – three! Fouled[5]! He launched himself high into space, stretched his arms and legs forward. Seven metres! He knew it! But that didn't count.

'Watch that board, boy,' the coach's words reached him from very far away. 'Come on, try again. Hurry, we don't have all day.'

He walked back on legs that felt like rubber. His heart was pounding inside his throat. Nervously, he brushed the sand off his elbow, and, still rubbing it, took position, bent forwards, eyes on the pit. The faces of the boys lining the narrow pit merged into a blurred[6] haze. He rose onto his toes, fell into a start, and pushed forward. The board! He had to mind the board. He didn't usually foul. Why did he now? Now, when it mattered. Three more steps, one more and ... foul! Yes, his shoes had touched the sand bordering the take-off board. There was no point stretching out to reach the seven-metre mark. But while his mind had resigned, his legs arched upwards, followed by his arms stretching forward in a parallel line. Then he hit the ground, burying his forehead in the soft, cool, sand.

'What's the matter with you, boy?' The coach's voice wasn't unfriendly. 'Haven't you been taught how to count your steps? Come on, last try. Get moving.'

He picked himself up, hot with shame. From the sea of faces, he thought he heard a snigger[7].

How he wished he were back home, amongst his friends. They wouldn't laugh at him. There was no point trying again. He wouldn't make it. Not now, not here. No use going on. But his feet carried him on, back to the start. He stared at the board, without actually seeing it because something buzzed inside his head, hammered against his temples with great force. He knew he couldn't jump.

Just then he felt a hand on his shoulder and a face appeared before him. He saw someone's lips moving, curving up into a smile. Rattan Mehta! He was telling

Wordfile

5. In a sport, if someone **fouls**, they do something that is not allowed according to the rules.
6. Something that is **blurred** is not clear.
7. A **snigger** is a quiet, unkind laugh.

him something. What was he saying? He concentrated hard, really hard, staring at the red sweater in Rattan Mehta's hands. 'Those were two fantastic jumps,' Rattan Mehta nodded, 'seven metres, no kidding[8]. We need someone like you. Here, why don't you use this as a landmark; put the sweater down a few inches away from the take-off mark. Why don't you try it?'

He followed him down to the pit, stared down at his back as he placed the sweater near the track. Nodding silently, he managed to croak. 'Thanks.'

A broad smile flashed over Rattan Mehta's face. 'V for victory,' he said, with a playful shove[9]. It was then that something snapped inside his head. The feeling of being paralysed ebbed away[10] and something started to vibrate inside and around him. Once more he got ready for the jump, his eyes on the pit, the red sweater near the take-off mark. He pushed hard into the sand, one - two - three. He lifted himself into the air, stretched forward and landed beautifully, on his knees.

Behind him rose an uproar[11] which swelled[12] into thunderous applause. He knew he had made it.

Sigrun Srivastav

Wordfile

8. If you say **no kidding**, you mean that you are serious about what you have just said. (*informal*)
9. A **shove** is a strong push.
10. If something **ebbs away**, it becomes less and less.
11. An **uproar** is a situation in which people are making a lot of noise.
12. If something **swells**, it increases in size or level.

About the author

Sigrun Srivastav (b. 1943) is an Indian author of German origin. She is an illustrator and writer of picture books, short stories, adventure books and family novels. Many of her stories are based on real-life incidents from around the world. She also writes extensively on social issues such as poverty, discrimination and the problems of the differently abled. Some of her published works are *No Time For Fear*, *Trapped*, *The Ghost Rider of Darbhanga* and *Grin and Bear it, Abhy*.

Comprehension 1

A **Arrange the sentences in the order of the events in the story.**

1. The boy did two jumps that were not allowed because his foot touched the sand. ______
2. The boy did a successful jump and the crowd clapped. ______
3. Rattan Mehta spoke to him and said how good his jumps were. ______
4. The boy thought Rattan Mehta and the other boys were laughing at him. ______
5. Rattan Mehta placed a red sweater by the take-off mark to help the boy know exactly where to jump from. ______

B **Answer the questions.**

1. How did the boy try to prepare himself for his jump?
2. How did the author describe Rattan Mehta?
3. What did he think the boys around the long-jump pit were doing?
4. After the warm-up run, what did the boy wish?
5. After his second failed jump, the boy stood up 'hot with shame'. What did he think he heard at this point?
6. When Rattan Mehta came over to speak to the boy, two lines in the story tell us that the boy could not hear what he was saying. What are those lines?

C **Read the lines and answer the questions.**

1. 'He knew he could beat them, all of them – but he wouldn't.'

   This is the second line of the story. The boy clearly knew that he was good at long-jump, yet he felt he would not succeed that day. Why?
2. 'Watch that board, boy,' the coach's words reached him from very far away. 'Come on, try again. Hurry, we don't have all day.'

   The coach spoke to the boy on several occasions. What was he like? How did he treat the boys?
3. 'It was then that something snapped inside his head.'

   Does this line describe something good or something bad? What does it mean?
4. 'He lifted himself into the air, stretched forward and landed beautifully, on his knees.'

   What happened after this?

Comprehension 2

Answer the questions.

1. This story describes in detail how the boy felt before the competition. He had no confidence and he was sure that he would fail. Why do you think he felt this way?
2. We see the experience of taking part in a competition through the boy's eyes. This means we see the events as the boy imagines them to be happening, though in reality, things might be quite different. Find examples of feelings, descriptions and events in the story that you think are probably not true.
3. VBQ Success is as dependent on talent as it is on self belief. Do you agree with the statement? Give reasons for your answer.

Vocabulary

Word meanings

A Complete the definition of the word or phrase in bold using the words in the box.

stand	weigh	push	jump	curved	hand	ground	weak

1. 'He fell into a warm-up run, conscious of his legs **growing heavy** as lead ...'

   If your legs grow heavy, you start to feel as if they ____________ a lot.

2. 'He walked back on legs that **felt like rubber**.'

   If your legs feel like rubber, they start to feel ____________ and walking becomes difficult.

3. 'He **picked himself up**, hot with shame.'

   If you pick yourself up, you ____________ up with difficulty.

4. 'He lifted himself into the air, stretched forward and **landed** beautifully, on his knees.'

   If you land somewhere, you come down to the ____________ after moving through the air.

5. 'The coach collected the boys with a **sweeping gesture** of his arm.'

   If you make a sweeping gesture, you make a big movement with your ____________.

6. 'He **launched himself** high into space, stretched his arms and legs forward.'

   If you launch yourself, you ____________ with great energy.

7. '... his legs **arched** upwards, followed by his arms stretching forward ...'

   If a part of your body arches, it makes a ____________ shape.

8. 'A broad smile flashed over Rattan Mehta's face. "V for victory," he said, with a playful **shove**.'

   If you give someone a shove, you ____________ them roughly.

B **Write the correct verbs next to their meaning.**

merge	snap	vibrate	sprint	pound	stare

1. to run very fast ____________
2. the heart beating fast and forcefully, often as a result of shock or fear ____________
3. to combine two things to become one ____________
4. to look at someone or something for a long time ____________
5. to break with a short sharp sound ____________
6. to shake with repeated small, quick movements ____________

C **Which sports do these words relate to: cricket, football or running? Put the words in the correct column. Some words may be placed in multiple columns.**

bowl someone out	fire the gun	batting	free kick	goal	hurdle
kick-off	lap	marathon	over (*noun*)	penalty	pitch
sprint	starting line	bowler	stumps	wicket	off-side

cricket	football	running

D **Write the opposites of these words from the story.**

1. best	________	5. broad	________
2. conscious	________	6. nervous	________
3. handsome	________	7. swelled	________
4. encouraging	________	8. forward	________

Grammar

Active and passive voice

Look at this sentence.

***He** wished he hadn't come to Delhi.*

Here, the subject, ***He***, is the 'performer' of the action. When the subject of a sentence is the performer of the action, it is said to be in the **active voice**.

Sometimes, the subject is not the performer of the action. Instead, it is affected by the action.

***He** was laughed at by the other competitors.*

Here, the subject, ***He***, receives the action of the verb, ***was laughed at***. When the subject of a sentence is the recipient of the action of the verb, it is said to be in the **passive voice**.

Passive voice is used when the focus of the sentence is on the action and not the performer of the action. To make a passive sentence, you use the structure **to be + past participle** of the main verb. The preposition ***by*** introduces the person or thing that does the action.

Sometimes, the performer of the action is not mentioned. This is usually done when:

- the performer of the action is not known
  The fence between the two houses was removed.
- the performer of the action is not important
  Valuable items should be kept in the safe.
- people in general are the performers of the action
  Both the books can be found in any library.
- the performer of the action has already been mentioned
  The police responded immediately and the suspects were arrested.

A **Change the sentences from active to passive voice. Use the word *by* when mentioning the performer of the action.**

1. My teacher told me to read the book.
   I was told to read the book by my teacher.
2. Fire damaged the city centre.
   The city centre was ____________________
3. Farhan Akhtar directed the film.
   The film ____________________
4. A child of twelve wrote the book.
   The book ____________________
5. My grandfather built this house.
   This ____________________
6. Christopher Columbus discovered America.
   ____
7. Alexander Bell invented the telephone.
   ____
8. Manya taught me how to swim.
   ____
9. The wizard defeated the evil magician in a duel.
   ____

B **Rearrange the words to make meaningful sentences. Then identify if they are in the active or the passive voice.**

1. was born/my father/in Mumbai
   My father was born in Mumbai. (passive)
2. in the accident/was injured/luckily, no one
3. played all over/football is/the world
4. down in/the tree/the storm/was blown
5. to the wrong/the parcel/address/was sent
6. your home/will be/the books/sent to
7. was written/this poem/by Tagore
8. a singer/was won by/from Mumbai/the contest
9. Batman is/the identity of/in Gotham/known to very/few people

C **Complete the sentences using the passive form of these verbs.**

announce steal disturb import build cancel

1. The school ______________ ten years ago.
2. The winner of the competition will be ______________ next Tuesday.
3. I hope you were not ______________ by all the noise.
4. The match was ______________ because of the bad weather.
5. I forgot to lock my bike and, unfortunately, it ______________.
6. A lot of fruit is ______________ into the UK.

Articles

Look at these sentences.

I know ***the*** *boy who was selected as school captain.*

We were looking for ***a*** *boy to play the role of the king in the play.*

In the first sentence, the definite article *the* has been used. In the second sentence, the indefinite article *a* has been used.

We use the indefinite articles **a** and **an** when we do not know the person or object being referred to. We use the definite article **the** to refer to persons or objects that we know about.

D **Rewrite the sentence inserting articles wherever required.**

1. Samir is youngest boy in class.
2. *The Bible* is holy book of Christians.
3. I live in bungalow. Bungalow is near my school.
4. My uncle has egg, apple and sandwich for breakfast.
5. Naseer is learning to play guitar.
6. I want to be engineer when I grow up.
7. Match ended in a draw after full time and both teams were awarded a point each.
8. King suspected minister of plotting against him and ordered chief of spies to gather proof of plot.
9. Many people believe that discovery of fire is most important event in history of mankind.
10. One of explanations for extinction of dinosaurs is meteor striking Earth.

Listening

Listening to interviews

A **Listen to two interviews with sportspersons just after they have taken part in a game or competition. Answer these questions.**

Interview 1

1. What has the cricketer just achieved?
2. How does the interviewer describe this achievement?
3. What disappointing thing happened to the cricketer?

Interview 2

4. Which words does the interviewer use to express her sympathy for the runner after she lost the race?
5. How did the runner prepare for the race?
6. When is the runner's next race?

B **Listen to the interviews again and complete the sentences.**

Interview 1

1. **Interviewer:** I suppose you were a bit disappointed to ________________ in the next over?
2. **Cricketer:** Yes, of course, but as you say, with bowling as strong as that, it was ________________.

Interview 2

3. **Interviewer:** Can you explain what happened?

   Runner: Not really, to be honest. It was going really well for the first 300 metres. I was ________________ and feeling strong, but then I lost a bit of speed in the last 50 metres or so, and I ________________ Murthy.

Speaking

Interviews

A **Imagine that you have competed in a match, a race or any other sporting event. If you have competed in a real sporting event, you could also think about that.**

Make notes about what happened (both good and bad), using the vocabulary you have learnt in this unit.

B **Work in pairs, with one student playing a sportsperson and the other playing a journalist. Use the notes you have made to enact an interview where the journalist asks the sportsperson about his/her experience of participating in a recently concluded sports event. The journalist should ask whether the sportsperson's team won or lost and offer his/her sympathy if the sportsperson has lost. She or he should also find out all about the event. Swap roles after ten questions.**

Useful phrases

Congratulations on a fantastic performance!

Well done!

Bad luck!

That was a fantastic/brilliant/very impressive performance!

You must be very pleased/delighted/thrilled with your performance!

You must be quite disappointed with that result.

You tried your best.

Luck was against you this time.

Better opportunities will come your way.

Setbacks make one more determined to succeed.

Can you explain what happened?

What happened there?

Why do you think that happened?

Writing

Read this report in a school newspaper on the institution's annual sports day.

Red House Wins Sports Championship Trophy After Five Years

The annual Sports Day of The World School was held on 14 January 2016 in the Gitanjali Stadium. It was a sunny Sunday morning.

The day started at 9 a.m. with an opening ceremony. First, the Principal, Mrs Swati Roy, gave a welcome speech and introduced the chief guest. Then, all the students sang the school song. Two students presented a bouquet of flowers and a memento to the chief guest, who declared the meet open.

The four Houses, Red House, Yellow House, Blue House and Green House, were present in full strength. The day's events included high jump, long jump, the 200-metre race, the 400-metre race, hurdles and relay race. The high point of the day was the high jump competition. Kalyani Sharma, a student of Class 9 from Yellow House broke the long jump record set by Class 11 student Preeta Moitra last year. The last event was the tug-of-war. Green House won this competition.

There were about 1200 students in the audience who cheered the participants.

Red House won the Championship Trophy. This was their first win in five years. Swarnila Sett, the Red House captain said, 'I dedicate our win to all the students who worked hard and gave their best to the team.'

Rohini Gupta,
School Captain

A Now, write a report about a sporting event for your school magazine.

You can use notes from page 118, or you might prefer to write about a different event. (It can be an event that you have watched on the television.)

Before you start, think about the following points:

- Who scored and when?
- How was their performance at the start of the match, during half-time and at the end of the day?
- What were the highlights (= best parts) of the match?
- Who gave the best performance in both teams?
- What was each team's main weakness/strength? (How was their defence/attack / bowling /batting, etc?)
- How do you think the team's manager might feel about their performance?

Poem

This poem is about a child's experience of playing football. Read the poem and notice all the words that relate to the sounds and emotions that the child hears and experiences.

One Look

As I stand on that muddy grass field,
The roar of the cheering crowds
Is all I seem to hear.
No specific voices, it's all just a blur[1].
The only person I really notice,
Is the yelling of my coach.

As I go to challenge the ball,
I think, 'I want my coach to be proud of me.'
The ball is at my feet, I have to be quick.
I dribble[2] up the side of the field,
Cut in and cross, one touch,
From another player, and Goal!
I know my coach is proud of me,
From just one look.

Walking to the car,
Ball in hand, covered all in mud,
I receive compliments on a great game.
I say thanks, but all that matters,
After the game-winning goal,
Is that one look from my coach.

Ashley

Wordfile

1. If things around you are **just a blur**, you do not see or hear them clearly.
2. In a sport, if you **dribble**, you keep a ball moving by using your hand or foot.

Poetry appreciation

Answer the questions.

1. Which of these is most important to the football player in the poem?
   a. what the cheering crowd thinks about how well he has played
   b. how well he thinks he has played
   c. what the coach thinks about how well he has played
2. Which two words tell you about the noises at the football match?
3. What does the phrase, 'it's all just a blur', mean? Why is it 'all just a blur' for this player?

4. What does the 'one look' in the title of this poem refer to? When does it happen?
5. What do people say to the player as he walks to the car?
6. What do you think is more important to a player: appreciation from the coach, love from the spectators or both? Give reasons for your answer. VBQ

Activity

A **Work with a partner and find the following information about the 2016 Summer Olympics.**

Host city: ____________________

Date: ____________________

Number of sports: ____________________

Number of events in each category: ____________________

Number of venues: ____________________

Number of participating countries: ____________________

B **How many medals did India win at the 2016 Olympics and in which categories? Write the names of the winners.**

What was noteworthy about the winners as a group?

C **Do you know what the logo of the Olympic Games is? Draw it in the space below.**

Do you know what the logo symbolizes? Find out and write down the significance of the five rings.

6 Looking Back and Looking Forwards

In this unit, I will ...

- learn some prefixes and suffixes
- practise homonyms and parts of speech
- learn how to use conditional sentences for talking about imaginary situations
- listen to people talking about time travel and share my own ideas on the topic
- write a diary entry

Warm-up

A Work with a partner. Look at these predictions that people made about what would happen in the future. Note that they were made a long time ago.

1. Have any of them come true yet?
2. How many of these do you think are probable in future?

Cars will drive themselves.

We will grow bigger fruits and vegetables that will feed more people.

There will be no more cars in cities. Vehicles will travel under the ground instead.

Computers will become so clever that they will be able to beat the world's best human chess player.

B Make a few predictions of your own about the future and share them with your partner.

Reading 1

Read the text below quickly and tick [✓] the option that you think best describes the theme of the text.

1. This text is about predictions in the past that came true. [ ]
2. This text is about predictions in the past that did not come true. [ ]
3. This text is about some predictions in the past that came true and some that did not. [ ]

Science Fiction or Science Facts?

How would you feel if you were told that the mobile phone, the tablet, the touch-screen television, satellite communication, space travel, submarines, the Internet, the atomic bomb, and even pre-packaged foods, were once only ideas in books called 'science fiction' or 'sci-fi', and while people read about them with a lot of interest, they didn't think these would ever come true?

Surprised?

Having the world at our fingertips is something that we take for granted today. However, even 150 years ago, things that we consider everyday objects today, such as aeroplanes, cars, telephone, radio and even television did not exist.

How, then, did all this come about?

The answer is human imagination. In fact, human imagination is the basis of all human progress, because human beings are always looking for ways to increase their knowledge and make life easier and better.

When such ideas come to inventors, or people who have scientific knowledge, they work on them and turn them into reality. However, when these ideas for scientific inventions occur to people who are not trained to work on them and turn them into reality, they take the form of science fiction, or 'sci-fi'. Jules Verne, H. G. Wells, Arthur C. Clarke and Aldous Huxley were some of the most famous sci-fi writers of the nineteenth and twentieth

centuries. Many of the predictions that they made in their books and articles are today's realities.

Jules Verne: rocket ships

In 1865, Jules Verne wrote *From the Earth to the Moon*, one of the earliest examples of modern science fiction. In this, more than 100 years before man actually landed on the moon, he made surprisingly perfect predictions about lunar modules[1], solar sails[2] and humans landing on the moon.

Arthur C. Clarke: satellite communication, space tourism, online newspapers and the tablet computer

Sci-fi legend[3] Arthur C. Clarke wrote about communications satellites in *Wireless World* a full ten years before their actual development.

In the 1968 film *2001: A Space Odyssey*, based on Clarke's novel of the same name, two astronauts can be seen reading a newspaper on something called the 'Newspad', which looks very much like the modern-day tablet. They are seen to call up the world's major electronic papers by punching in their suggestions.

Space tourism[4] was another feature of the movie, which has now become a reality. Just as in the film, fee-paying passengers can now actually travel to the International Space Station. Private companies are taking bookings for sub-orbital[5] and orbital spaceflights. In the longer term, hotels in space and even visits to the moon are planned.

Raymond Kurzweil: wireless Internet, nanotechnology, e-books and more

Raymond Kurzweil, of Google, has invented text-reading software and written five bestselling novels. He has made dozens of scientific predictions with unbelievable accuracy.

For instance, in his novel *The Age of Intelligent Machines*, Kurzweil predicted a computer beating the best human players at chess by the year 2000, and wireless Internet becoming practical for normal everyday use in the early twenty-first century.

In *The Age of Spiritual Machines*, he predicted e-books, face recognition software[6] and nanotechnology[7].

Wordfile

1. The **Lunar Module** was a spacecraft which carried men to and from the Moon during the 1960s and 1970s.
2. **Solar sails** are a way of making spacecraft move forward.
3. A **legend** is a person who is very famous and greatly admired.
4. **Space tourism** is travel in space for the purpose of having holidays.
5. A **sub-orbital** flight is a trip into space in which the spacecraft does not go into orbit (= does not follow a curved path around Earth).
6. **Face-recognition software** is software (= computer programs) that recognizes a person from an image of their face.
7. **Nanotechnology** is an area of science in which atoms are controlled in order to produce materials, devices and machines.

H. G. Wells: the atomic bomb

In his novel *The World Set Free*, published in 1914, famous sci-fi writer H. G. Wells wrote about the atomic bomb and its destructive potential[8]. This came true in 1945 when the atomic bomb was dropped on Hiroshima and Nagasaki in Japan, ending the Second World War.

Aldous Huxley: test tube babies and genetic engineering

Aldous Huxley's classic sci-fi novel *Brave New World* predicted the world in which we now live with amazing truth. The book has detailed descriptions of genetic engineering[9]: test tube babies[10], cloning[11], and genetic manipulation[12], which are now a part of our modern society.

So, can it truly be said that the science fiction of today is the scientific fact of tomorrow?

Wordfile

8. The **potential** of something or someone is the ability it has to do something in the future.
9. **Genetic engineering** is the process of changing the genes (= parts of a cell that control the characteristics of a living thing) in order to improve a living thing.
10. **Test tube baby** is an old-fashioned phrase for a baby that developed from an egg that was taken from the mother's body, joined with a male cell and then put inside the mother's body for the baby to grow.
11. **Cloning** is the activity of making a new but identical animal or plant from the cells of another animal or plant.
12. **Genetic manipulation** is the process of changing the genes (= parts of a cell that control the characteristics of a living thing) in order to improve a living thing.

Well, as we know, not all predictions come true. Here are some of the most impressive ones that went wrong:

- 'A rocket will never be able to leave the Earth's atmosphere.'

  The New York Times, 13 January, 1920.

  This was proved wrong when *Apollo 11* landed on the Moon on 20 July, 1969.

- 'There's no chance that the iPhone is going to get any significant market share.'

  Steve Ballmer, USA Today, 30 April, 2007

- 'Remote shopping, while entirely feasible, will flop.'

  Time Magazine, 1966

- 'Well-informed people know that it is impossible to transmit[13] the human voice over wires as may be done with dots and dashes of Morse code[14].

  A Boston newspaper, 1865

Parul Gupta

Wordfile

13. To **transmit** something is to send it from one place to another.
14. **Morse code** is a system for sending messages in which all the letters of the alphabet are represented using short and long sounds or flashes of light.

Comprehension 1

A Match the people in column A with the predictions that they made in column B.

A	B
1. Jules Verne	a. computer programs that recognize a person from an image of their face
2. Arthur C. Clarke	b. a moon landing
3. Ray Kurzweil	c. holidays in space
4. H. G. Wells	d. the making of new but identical animals or plants from the cells of other animals or plants
5. Aldous Huxley	e. an extremely powerful bomb

B **Answer the questions.**

1. What quality of the human beings, according to the author, has enabled them to make great progress in the field of science and technology?
2. According to the author, what are human beings always trying to do?
3. How do people without special knowledge of science propagate their ideas when new ideas come to them?

Comprehension 2

VBQ

1. 'Human beings are always looking for ways to [...] make life easier and better.'

   Is it always a good thing that people are looking for ways to make life easier and better? Do you think this may have some bad effects? Give reasons.
2. Many people predicted that certain scientific breakthroughs like super-fast trains could never be achieved. Yet, scientists have worked on those ideas and proven them wrong. What lesson do we learn from this?

Vocabulary check

Find words from the passage using these clues.

1. an idiom that means 'near us and available all the time': at ____________
2. an idiom that means 'to expect something and not appreciate how useful or valuable it really is': take ____________
3. a noun that means 'the most important part of something that other things can develop from': b ____________
4. a phrasal verb that means 'to start to happen': c ____________ a ____________
5. a noun that means 'real things rather than imagined ideas': r ____________
6. a noun in two parts that means 'books and films about things that happen in the future or in other parts of the universe': s ____________ f ____________
7. a two-part term that means 'how many products a company sells compared to how many similar products other companies sell': m ____________ s ____________

Language skills

Prefixes

A **prefix** is a group of letters at the beginning of a word. A prefix is used with a root word to form a new word.

*The instructions were **un**clear* (antonym of the root word ***clear***).

*I'm **un**certain (= not certain) about the arrangements.*

Other common prefixes are **under-** meaning 'below' (***under**water*), **re-**, meaning 'again' (***re**use* = to use again).

A **Look at the four sets of words. Each set contains words with a particular prefix. Match the prefixes with the meanings given in the box.**

between	earlier than	under	over a long distance

1. *prediction* *pre-packaged foods* *pre-heat* *pre-cook*
   meaning of prefix *pre-* __________
2. *sub-orbital* *submarines* *sub-zero temperatures*
   meaning of prefix *sub-* __________
3. *telephone* *television* *telegraph*
   meaning of prefix *tele-* __________
4. *international* *Internet* *interact* *interpret*
   meaning of prefix *inter-* __________

B **Use your dictionary to write two more words with each prefix from Exercise A.**

C **Add prefixes to form antonyms of the words given in brackets and complete the sentences.**

1. The __________ (honest) minister joined the enemy forces and plotted against the king.
2. Sakshi Malik's performance in the Rio Olympics was __________. (believable)
3. Viruses and bacteria are __________ (visible) to the naked eye.
4. Soham's attendance at school was __________ (regular) because he was often unwell.
5. Priya's __________ (kind) words hurt her friend.

A **suffix** is a group of letters at the end of a word. A suffix is used with a root word to form a new word.

Some suffixes have particular meanings. The suffix -**ful** means 'with a particular quality'.

*beauti**ful** (full of beauty)* *hope**ful** (full of hope)*

Other suffixes change the part of speech of a word.

*tire (verb) → tir**ed** (adjective)* *surprise (noun) → surpris**ed** (adjective)*

Suffixes like **-er**, **-or**, **-ist** and **-ian** are commonly used to form words related to professions.

*writ**er*** *invent**or*** *doct**or*** *psycholog**ist*** *politic**ian***

Suffixes

D Form the names of people who belong to these professions using suffixes. Then, place the names in the appropriate columns in the table below.

1. ~~someone who writes **novels** as a job~~
2. ~~someone who works in a **library**~~
3. someone who works in **science**
4. someone who mends **electrical** things
5. someone who creates works of **art**
6. someone who **designs** things
7. someone who works in the **reception** of an office or a hotel
8. someone who **directs** films
9. someone who **presents** programmes on television
10. someone who does **magic** tricks, often for children
11. someone who plays a **piano** professionally
12. someone who **edits** books
13. someone who studies or teaches **language**
14. someone who prepares medicines in a **pharmacy**
15. someone who **translates** languages
16. someone who creates **music**

-ist	-ian	-er	-or
novelist	librarian		

Reading 2

Many scientists search for signs of intelligent life in the Universe. As human beings, we tend to think ourselves as the most intelligent of all living creatures. What if there were other intelligent beings in faraway galaxies? How would you feel if you came to know that they did not want to be contacted by us because they thought humans to be *less* developed than them? Read this story about two such beings talking to each other about human beings who are trying to contact them.

About the author

Terry Bisson (b. 1942) is an American writer of science fiction. Some of his best-known stories are 'Bears Discover Fire' and 'macs'. He has won the Hugo and the Nebula, two of the biggest awards in science-fiction writing.

They're Made out of Meat

'They're made out of meat.'

'Meat?'

'Meat. They're made out of meat.'

'Meat?'

'There's no doubt about it. We picked up several from different parts of the planet, took them aboard our recon[1] vessels, and probed[2] them all the way through. They're completely meat.'

'That's impossible. What about the radio signals? The messages to the stars?'

'They use the radio waves to talk, but the signals don't come from them. The signals come from machines.'

'So who made the machines? That's who we want to contact.'

'They made the machines. That's what I'm trying to tell you. Meat made the machines.'

'That's ridiculous. How can meat make a machine? You're asking me to believe in sentient[3] meat.'

'I'm not asking you, I'm telling you. These creatures are the only sentient race in that sector and they're made out of meat.'

'Maybe they're like the orfolei. You know, a carbon-based intelligence that goes through a meat stage.'

Wordfile

1. **Recon** is an informal American word for 'reconnaissance'. It is the process of getting information about the position, activity, etc of someone who could be an enemy.
2. If you **probe** something, you examine it, especially with a long, thin instrument.
3. If someone is **sentient**, they can see or feel things through the senses.

'Nope. They're born meat and they die meat. We studied them for several of their life spans[4], which didn't take long. Do you have any idea what's the life span of meat?'

'Spare me. Okay, maybe they're only part meat. You know, like the weddilei. A meat head with an electron plasma[5] brain inside.'

'Nope. We thought of that, since they do have meat heads, like the weddilei. But I told you, we probed them. They're meat all the way through.'

'No brain?'

'Oh, there's a brain all right. It's just that the brain is made out of meat! That's what I've been trying to tell you.'

'So ... what does the thinking?'

'You're not understanding, are you? You're refusing to deal with what I'm telling you. The brain does the thinking. The meat.'

'Thinking meat! You're asking me to believe in thinking meat!'

'Yes, thinking meat! Conscious meat! Loving meat. Dreaming meat. The meat is the whole deal! Are you beginning to get the picture or do I have to start all over?'

'Oh my God. You're serious then. They're made out of meat.'

'Thank you. Finally. Yes. They are indeed made out of meat. And they've been trying to get in touch with us for almost a hundred of their years.'

'Oh my God. So what does this meat have in mind?'

'First, it wants to talk to us. Then I imagine it wants to explore the Universe, contact other sentiences, swap[6] ideas and information. The usual.'

'We're supposed to talk to meat.'

'That's the idea. That's the message they're sending out by radio. 'Hello. Anyone out there. Anybody home.' That sort of thing.'

Wordfile

4. Someone's **life span** is the length of time they are likely to live for under normal conditions.
5. **Plasma** is a gas that has equal numbers of positive and negative electric charges. It is present in the sun and most stars.
6. If you **swap** somthing, you give it to someone in return for something else.

Wordfile

7. If you **squirt** something, you force it out of a narrow opening.
8. A **quadrant** is a quarter of a circle.
9. **Prejudice** is, usually, a negative opinion that is formed without knowing the facts adequately.
10. If something is **infinitesimal**, it is extremely small.

'They actually do talk, then. They use words, ideas, concepts?'

'Oh, yes. Except they do it with meat.'

'I thought you just told me they used radio.'

'They do, but what do you think is on the radio? Meat sounds. You know how when you slap or flap meat, it makes a noise? They talk by flapping their meat at each other. They can even sing by squirting[7] air through their meat.'

'Oh my God. Singing meat. This is altogether too much. So what do you advise?'

'Officially or unofficially?'

'Both.'

'Officially, we are required to contact, welcome and log in any and all sentient races or multibeings in this quadrant[8] of the Universe, without prejudice[9], fear or favour. Unofficially, I advise that we erase the records and forget the whole thing.'

'I was hoping you would say that.'

'It seems harsh, but there is a limit. Do we really want to make contact with meat?'

'I agree one hundred percent. What's there to say? 'Hello, meat. How's it going?' But will this work? How many planets are we dealing with here?'

'Just one. They can travel to other planets in special meat containers, but they can't live on them. And being meat, they can only travel through C space. Which limits them to the speed of light and makes the possibility of their ever making contact pretty slim. Infinitesimal[10], in fact.'

'So we just pretend there's no one home in the Universe.'

'That's it.'

'Cruel. But you said it yourself, who wants to meet meat?

And the ones who have been aboard our vessels, the ones you probed? You're sure they won't remember?'

'They'll be considered crackpots if they do. We went into their heads and smoothed out their meat so that we're just a dream to them.'

'A dream to meat! How strangely appropriate, that we should be meat's dream.'

'And we marked the entire sector unoccupied.'

'Good. Agreed, officially and unofficially. Case closed. Any others? Anyone interesting on that side of the galaxy?'

'Yes, a rather shy but sweet hydrogen core cluster intelligence[11] in a class nine star in G445 zone. Was in contact two galactic rotations ago, wants to be friendly again.'

'They always come around.'

'And why not? Imagine how unbearably, how unutterably cold the Universe would be if one were all alone ...'

Terry Bisson

Wordfile

11. **Cluster intelligence** is a single collective intelligence that may be present in a number of bodies. The individual organisms often display complete lack of individual identities and exist as an intelligent being only in cluster.

Comprehension 1

Answer the questions.

1. What do you think the orfolei and the weddilei are? What do the speakers say about them?
2. How long had human beings been trying to contact them? Why?
3. What device did human beings use to contact them?
4. Which characteristic feature of human beings surprised the speakers the most? According to one of the speakers, how did human beings speak and sing?

5. 'And being meat, they can only travel through C space.'
   What happened because humans could only travel through C space?
6. Officially, what did the speakers have to do if intelligent beings from other planets contacted them?
7. What had one of the speakers done to make sure that the human beings who had boarded their vessels didn't remember anything?
8. What other signs of intelligent life did the speakers find in the galaxy?

Comprehension 2

Answer the questions.

1. How do we realise that the beings who had tried to contact the speakers were human beings?
2. Why don't the speakers want to make contact with human beings?
3. VBQ Do you think that the speakers' attitude to human beings is similar to our attitude towards animals and organisms we consider less intelligent than us?
4. VBQ What lesson does the story teach us?

Vocabulary

Homonyms

A Complete the following sets of sentences with homonyms from the story. Then, write the meaning of the word in each case.

Remember: Homonyms are words with the same spelling and sound but different meanings.

1. a. I need more __________ to keep my luggage. Can you please move your suitcase a little?
   b. Human beings have always wondered whether there was life in outer __________
2. a. Ajay practised hard throughout the year, because he wanted to win the annual 400-metre __________
   b. The ancient Egyptians were a very advanced __________
3. a. Indian households usually use steel __________
   b. The *Mary-Anne* was one of the oldest __________ belonging to the shipping company.

4. a. Smita went up to the ________ confidently and began her speech.
   b. The scientists are in the final ________ of testing the new life-saving drug.
5. a. The businessmen struck a ________ which was satisfactory for both of them.
   b. I can't ________ with people who won't listen to reason.
6. a. A ship's captain has to maintain a daily ________ of all activities.
   b. Chris's father built a ________ cabin for his family where they would go every year during the summer break.

Parts of speech

B Complete the sentences with the noun form of the given words from the story.

shy   imagine   galactic   conscious   explore   live   agreed

1. Human beings have always had a thirst for ____________. Among such people, one of the most well-known is Christopher Columbus.
2. After a long discussion, the team members came to an ____________
3. Use your ____________ and write an article on what life would be like in the year 2050.
4. The patient regained ____________ after two days in hospital.
5. There are many undiscovered planets in every ____________
6. She could not make friends easily because of her ____________
7. Former Mr Universe Manohar Aich had a very long ________. He lived for 103 years.

Grammar

The second conditional

When we talk about the future result of a possible action or event, we use a simple **if**-clause.

They'll be considered crackpots if they do.

This type of structure is sometimes called the first conditional.

We use the **second conditional** when we are imagining a particular situation and saying what the result might be.

If I won *a lot of money, I* ***would*** *give a lot of it to charity.*

If you ***had*** *a bike, you* ***could*** *come cycling with us.*

Notice that you can use the second conditional to talk about something that is impossible (or extremely unlikely) or something that is possible but is not true at the time of speaking.

There are two clauses in a conditional sentence. One clause contains the word **If + a verb** in the simple past tense.

If *I* ***won*** *a lot of money, ...*

The other clause contains the word *would*, *could* or *might*.

... I ***would*** *give a lot of it to charity.*

Notice that you can change the order of the sentence parts so that the **if**-clause comes second.

You could come cycling with us if you had a cycle.

When the **if**-clause comes first, a comma is used to separate the two parts of the sentence.

If I had a time machine, I would travel to the future.

A **Match the first half of these conditional sentences with the second half.**

1. If you had a bicycle,	a. you could call him.
2. If I had more money,	b. I would make sure no one was hungry.
3. If you studied harder,	c. you would get there more quickly.
4. If you knew his telephone number,	d. you would get better grades at school.
5. If I could change one thing in the world,	e. I would buy a better cricket bat.

B **Which of these second conditional sentences are correct? Write *C* (correct) or *W* (wrong). Then, rewrite the wrong sentences correctly.**

1. If Feroze left our school, I would be really sad. ________

____

2. If I would have more money, I would buy more clothes. ________

____

3. If you told him the truth, he is really sad. ________

____

4. If we went by train, we would get there quicker. ________

____

5. Grandma would be very happy if you called her. ________

____

6. I would be very upset if my father forgets my birthday! ________

____

C Complete these sentences in the second conditional, using the correct tense of the verbs in brackets.

1. If I ________________ (*live*) in England, I ________________ (*eat*) fish and chips every day.
2. If I ________________ (*have*) more free time, I ________________ (*learn*) another language.
3. If I ________________ (*go*) to New York, I ________________ (*visit*) the Statue of Liberty.
4. If we ________________ (*not have*) so much homework, I ________________ (*go out*).
5. If I ________________ (*can*) choose, I ________________ (*travel*) into the future.
6. If there ________________ (*be*) fewer cars on the road, there ________________ (*not be*) so many accidents.

Prepositions

D Fill in the blanks with suitable prepositions.

1. I stayed up reading ________________ three in the morning.
2. Pat usually goes to school ________________ bus.
3. It has been raining ________________ morning.
4. My best friend's birthday is ________________ August.
5. She is one of the richest people ________________ the planet.
6. They are going ________________ a holiday next month.
7. The cat was waiting ________________ the mouse just ________________ its hole.
8. The man dived ________________ the sea in search ________________ the lost treasure.

Listening

Time travel

A **Travelling back and forth in time is one of the most commonly explored themes in science fiction. Listen to three young people talking about the time period they would like to travel to and circle the period that they are talking about.**

1. a. 2000 BCE b. 2045 c. 1970s/1980s
2. a. 2000 BCE b. 2045 c. 1970s/1980s
3. a. 2000 BCE b. 2045 c. 1970s/1980s

B **Listen to the three speakers again and complete the sentences.**

1. If I ____________ travel to any period I liked, I ____________ probably go back to the time when my parents were children.

   It would be so ____________ to see them all. And I would be so ____________ to see their parents – my grandparents – as young adults.
2. If I could travel forwards or backwards in time, I think I would choose thirty years from now. There are so many interesting ____________ in science and technology at the moment – in the ____________ of communication and medicine, for example.
3. If I could travel to any time period, I would ____________ go back – quite a long way back. I've always been interested in history, especially ____________ history, so I'd like to experience what life was like for people in those ancient civilizations when everything was so much simpler.

Speaking

A **Work with a partner. Make some notes about the good things that you could experience and achieve by travelling to another time period. Include any problems that you might experience too. Then, tell your partner about your ideas.**

Consider the answers to these questions while making your notes.

1. How would people from another time period respond to you? Would they accept you?
2. What would you take with you in your time machine?
3. If you went back in time, would you help people by warning them about bad things that would happen in the future?
4. If you went back in time, would you change anything you have done?

Use the highlighted phrases to help you.

Useful phrases

I **could** lose my time machine and not be able to return.
I **might** make good friends in the new time period and not want to leave them.
The people **might** not like me.
I **would probably** feel very homesick.
I **might possibly** meet myself as a younger child/older person.
I **would almost certainly** miss my family.
There's a chance I could change the course of history.
There's a possibility I might land in the middle of an ocean in my time machine.
I expect I would miss my family and friends.

Writing

A day on another planet

Imagine that you have travelled to another planet and you are now writing a diary entry.

Describe what you have been doing and what the world is like around you. Consider including information on these subjects:

- the building where you are staying
- the appearance of the city around you
- the transport that people use
- what the inhabitants eat
- where they sleep
- what they wear
- the technology that the inhabitants are using
- how you are feeling

You can write your diary entry on the next page.

22 September, 2017

09.00 a.m.

Dear Diary,

Tips for diary entries

Remember that you usually start a diary entry by giving the date and time.

Next, you mention the place where you are while writing the diary entry.

You can then describe what you have been doing that day or what you have noticed on that particular day. Try to include plenty of details.

Also, remember to include information about your emotions. Are you happy, excited, nervous or sad?

Here is an example:

Dear Diary,

It's Thurday, 2 September, 2200, and I'm sitting here on the 300th floor of the tallest building I've ever seen. Today has been the strangest day of my life. I've seen things today that you can't possibly imagine ...

Poem

Read this poem describing the poet's idea about what planet Earth was like millions of years ago.

The Bad Old Days

When Earth was a young planet spinning in space,
it certainly was a more dangerous place,
with hot molten lava[1] that flowed far and wide,
and meteors[2] falling but no place to hide.

It's good that we missed it - we could've been smashed!
The thunder was frightening, the lightning bolts[3] flashed,
as tidal waves[4] surged[5] from the pull of the moon,
and rain tumbled down in an endless monsoon.

When continents slowly rose from the sea,
the landscape was rocky - as bare as could be,
without any green plants or creatures that crawl,
since Earth at that time had no life forms at all.

The breezes were toxic[6], the volcanoes smoked,
the air was so poisonous, we would've choked[7]!
A billion years later (it's hard to say when),
bacteria[8] started to make oxygen.

The life forms were simple, but slowly they grew,
then cells joined together to makes something new -
since those early ages when Earth was ablaze[9],
life has evolved[10] in spectacular ways!

Loreen Leedy

Wordfile

1. **Lava** is the very hot liquid rock that comes out of a volcano.
2. A **meteor** is a piece of rock from outer space that makes a bright line across the night sky as it burns up while falling through the earth's atmosphere.
3. A **lightning bolt** is a very bright flash of light in the sky that happens during a storm.
4. A **tidal wave** is a very large wave, often caused by an earthquake.
5. If something **surges** somewhere, it moves in that direction with a lot of power.
6. Something that is **toxic** is poisonous.
7. If someone **chokes**, they cannot breathe because there is not enough air, or because something is blocking their throat.
8. **Bacteria** are very small living things that can be found everywhere.
9. Something that is **ablaze** is burning quickly and strongly.
10. If something **evolves**, it changes over a long period of time and gradually turns into something else.

About the poet

Loreen Leedy is an author-illustrator with over 40 published picture books on maths, science, language, arts and other curriculum topics. Some of her works are *Seeing Symmetry, My Teacher Is a Dinosaur, The Shocking Truth about Energy, Crazy Like a Fox, Fraction Action* and *Measuring Penny*. Her books have received several awards including the American Library Association Notable Book Award; the Chicago Library Best of the Best Award, the Florida Book Award and the Parents' Choice Award.

Poetry appreciation

Answer the questions.

1. There are five verses (= parts) in the poem. Each verse has a slightly different subject. Write the numbers of the verses 1–5 next to the subjects below.
   a. storms and water ________
   b. the way life developed over millions of years ________
   c. pieces of rock falling to Earth, and volcanoes ________
   d. the appearance of the land ________
   e. the atmosphere ________
2. The poem mentions two very bad things that would have happened to people if they had been on Earth during this period. What are those two things?
3. Which line tells you about the dangers coming from the sea?
4. Which words in the poem refer to heat and fire?
5. In the poem, there are a lot of words that describe the ways things move. Use your dictionary to match these verbs of movement in column A with their meanings in column B.

A	B
1. spin	a. to fall with a rolling movement
2. crawl	b. to move somewhere in a steady and continuous way
3. flow	c. to move upwards
4. rise	d. to turn quickly around a central point
5. tumble	e. to move slowly on your hands and knees

6. Compare the present day world with the one the poet has described.
7. When we talk about the past, we usually refer to it as the 'good old days'. Why do you think the poet is referring to the past as the 'bad old days'?

Activity

Work in small groups. Design a device or a robot with a particular function. Your invention may be realistic, or not realistic at all.

Use your notebook to draw a picture of your invention, remembering to label its different parts. Write a paragraph describing the function of your invention.

Here are a few ideas to help you:

- a childcare robot
- a robot that hangs up your clothes
- a cloak that makes you invisible
- an artificial eye
- a car that parks itself
- a car that flies
- an elevator that takes you into space

Useful phrases

Imagine how wonderful it would be if you could ...
Imagine not having to ...
This machine/device does it all for you!
Instead of having to ..., you simply ...
Basically, this machine/device will allow you to ...
When you press the button, it ...
When you pull the lever, it ...
This allows you to ...

A timeline

Do you know what a timeline is used for?

A timeline shows significant events in the past and those that are happening in the present. Sometimes it may also show planned events that are likely to happen at a particular time in the future.

A Look at this timeline. It shows important events in space history.

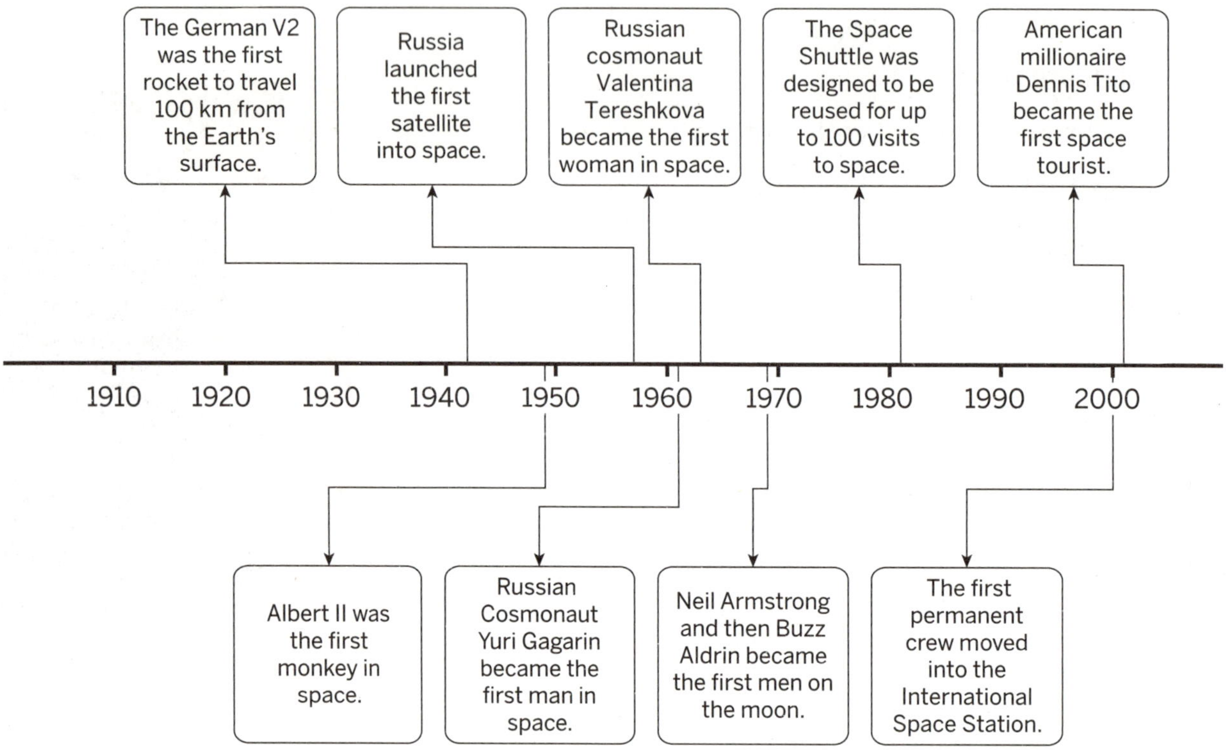

B Now look at these inventions. They were all invented in the twentieth century.

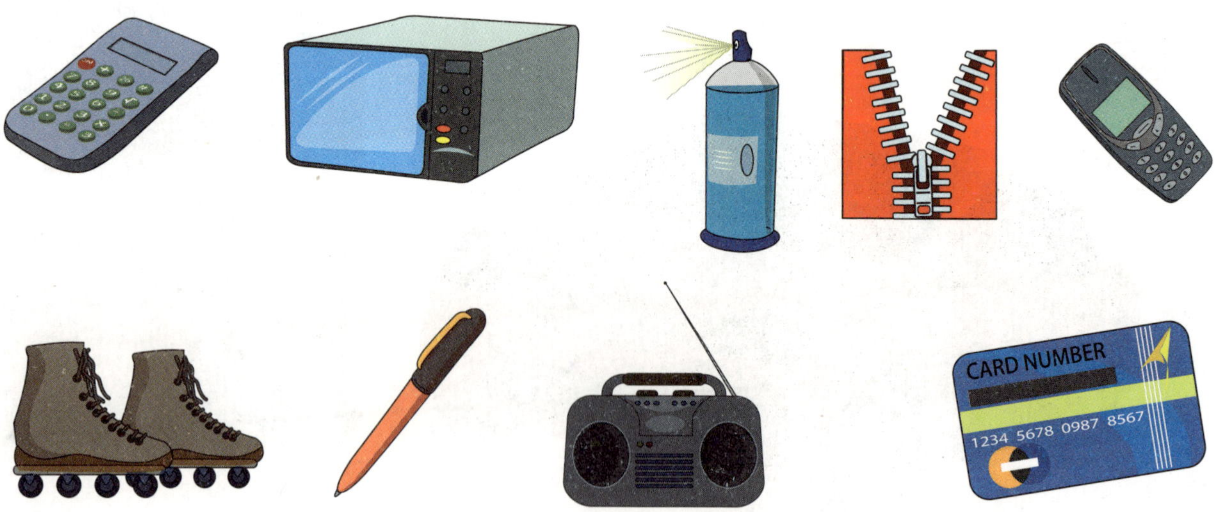

Find out the year when each of these was invented and write its name in the correct place in the timeline. Write the name of the inventor beside each invention too.

1910	1920	1930	1940	1950	1960	1970	1980	1990	2000

C Find out about four more inventions. Draw a picture of each invention in the boxes. Write their names, the year in which they were invented and the name of the inventor in the space given.

D In your notebook, draw a timeline of your life showing events which you think are important. You might include the following information:

- the year you were born
- when you started walking
- a year when a brother or sister was born
- the year you started going to school
- a year when you moved house
- a year when you won something

Your timeline could also feature your present-time activities. For example, when you moved to Class 6, and one or two projections for your future.

After you have prepared your timeline, compare it with one that a classmate has done.

- Do you and your partner have any years in common?
- Which events happened in those years?

Sports and sportsmanship

A The Annual Sports Day is in a week's time and students are busy practising for the various events. Asmita is a very competitive athlete and always performs well.

Unfortunately, she sprains her ankle during one of the practice sessions. The doctor prescribes complete rest for two days. Asmita is an important member of her school basketball team and she knows that if she does not play, her team might lose the game.

What should she do? Should she:

1. ignore the doctor's advice and continue practising? ☐
2. rest for one day and practise harder after that to make up? ☐
3. opt out of the game so that she is not part of her team's defeat? ☐
4. rest for a few days and then play the game, doing her best and not thinking about the results? ☐
5. blame herself for not being careful while practising and stop playing altogether to punish herself? ☐
6. request that the school authorities postpone the game until a later date? ☐

Which of the following are true for you? Discuss your answers with a partner.

1. I participate actively in sports. ☐
2. I represent my school in some sports. ☐
3. I like watching sports programmes on television. ☐
4. I am interested in seeing a sports event only if my school/region/country is taking part in it. ☐

B It is not only important to participate in sports, but also to have a good sportsmanlike attitude.

Imagine that you are taking part in a race in a school sports event. You have trained very hard, and you are determined to win.

During the race, you run very fast and cross the finishing line along with another participant.

You feel sure that you have won the race, but the referee announces that the other participant won by a slight margin. You are unhappy with this decision.

What would you do? Would you:

1. storm off because you think this decision is wrong? ☐
2. refuse to accept the medal for second place to show you are unhappy? ☐
3. talk to the other authorities to find out if the referee has given the correct decision? ☐
4. demand that the race be conducted again because you believe you have come first? ☐
5. accept the referee's decision and be happy about the fact that you won something? ☐

Discuss your answers in class.

NOTES

NOTES

NOTES

Collins Revised Exploring English 6

This revised edition of ***Exploring English*** is a multi-skill course that focuses on all aspects of language learning to help learners develop communicative competence. The syllabus for the series is designed to meet the requirements of the latest National Curriculum Framework. It offers high-quality English language materials to CBSE schools with clearly defined learning objectives. The series has been revised and updated based on user feedback.

Key Features

- **Reading** and **Comprehension** cover a wide range of classic, contemporary and original texts by Indian and international authors, for developing key comprehension skills
- **Vocabulary** and **Language skills** encourage the use of dictionaries and enrich the learner's language
- **Grammar** builds language proficiency through a variety of graded tasks to ensure progressive learning
- **Listening** and **Speaking** tasks hone active listening skills and build confidence in speaking English fluently
- **Writing** tasks challenge the learners to explore new ways of expressing themselves creatively
- **Project** and **Life skills** pages encourage group work and aid in formative assessment
- The clear and accessible layout and design facilitates learning

The course comprises Coursebooks 1 to 8, Workbooks 1 to 8, Literature Readers 3 to 8, Teacher's Resource Books 1 to 8, and a DVD containing resources for teachers and interactive features for learners.

Dr K. Padmini Shankar is a Professor in the Department of ESL Studies at the English and Foreign Languages University, Hyderabad. She has taught at the undergraduate and post-graduate levels for over two decades. Her research interests include classroom-based research, teacher training and development, and teaching young learners.

Collins DigiSuite for Teachers

Collins DigiSuite is a digital solution for teachers. Each DVD contains four components delivering classroom content that can be used to effectively integrate teaching and evaluation tools with the Coursebooks.

- **Multimedia e-book with animations, video snippets, presentations and interactive features**
- **Test Generator for quick test paper creation**
- **Teacher's Resource Books with answer keys, lesson plans and worksheets**
- **A PDF of the Collins dictionary appropriate for each level**

www.collins.in

₹580

ISBN 978-93-5277-139-4

9 789352 771394